a	i	u	e	o
a	ア	イ	ウ	エ	オ
k	カ (ka)	キ (ki)	ク (ku)	ケ (ke)	コ (ko)
s	サ (sa)	シ (shi)	ス (su)	セ (se)	ソ (so)
t	タ (ta)	チ (chi)	ツ (tsu)	テ (te)	ト (to)
n	ナ (na)	ニ (ni)	ヌ (nu)	ネ (ne)	ノ (no)
h	ハ (ha)	ヒ (hi)	フ (fu)	ヘ (he)	ホ (ho)
m	マ (ma)	ミ (mi)	ム (mu)	メ (me)	モ (mo)
y	ヤ (ya)		ユ (yu)		ヨ (yo)
r	ラ (ra)	リ (ri)	ル (ru)	レ (re)	ロ (ro)
w	ワ (wa)				ヲ (o)
n	ン (n)				

	kya	kyu	kyo
k	キャ	キュ	キョ
s	シャ (sha)	シュ (shu)	ショ (sho)
t	チャ (cha)	チュ (chu)	チョ (cho)
n	ニャ (nya)	ニュ (nyu)	ニョ (nyo)
h	ヒャ (hya)	ヒュ (hyu)	ヒョ (hyo)
m	ミャ (mya)	ミュ (myu)	ミョ (myo)
r	リャ (rya)	リュ (ryu)	リョ (ryo)

	ga	gi	gu	ge	go
g	ガ	ギ	グ	ゲ	ゴ
z	ザ (za)	ジ (ji)	ズ (zu)	ゼ (ze)	ゾ (zo)
d	ダ (da)	ヂ (ji)	ヅ (zu)	デ (de)	ド (do)
b	バ (ba)	ビ (bi)	ブ (bu)	ベ (be)	ボ (bo)
p	パ (pa)	ピ (pi)	プ (pu)	ペ (pe)	ポ (po)

	gya	gyu	gyo
g	ギャ	ギュ	ギョ
z	ジャ (ja)	ジュ (ju)	ジョ (jo)
b	ビャ (bya)	ビュ (byu)	ビョ (byo)
p	ピャ (pya)	ピュ (pyu)	ピョ (pyo)

NIHONGO ACTIVE TALK

The First Japanese Textbook for Beginners

上原由美子
UEHARA Yumiko

菊池民子
KIKUCHI Tamiko

ask PUBLISHING

About This Book

"I study Japanese, so I want to be able to be confident and enjoy engaging in conversation". We think many learners think this. But there are few people who can take on the challenge of real-life conversation soon after beginning their studies. For a variety of reasons—they have just started studying, they need to learn more vocabulary and grammar, they do not have self-confidence yet—many people satisfy themselves with brief interactions with the classroom teacher and classmates.

This textbook is a generalized learning tool with a focus on conversational Japanese tailored to the beginning student. Even if you have a small vocabulary or do not know proper grammar, you can still sufficiently carry on a conversation with a native Japanese speaker, provided you study and prepare the most basic expressions necessary, and you have the right environment. You will then sometimes succeed and sometimes fail, but it will always be a learning experience.

We certainly hope you find self-confidence through this textbook and enjoy conversing in Japanese.

Unit Content

①**Goals**   The goals of the unit. These correspond to the checkpoints at the end of each unit.

②**Short Dialogues**   Short exchanges in specific settings. As you listen to the speakers, speak along and practice. Refer to the following Expressions as needed. The mark of smiley face means the dialogue contains expressions that are used when talking to friends, family, or other familiar people.

③**Expressions**   The expressions required for the unit. These have been arranged to help you understand the Short Dialogues and so you can refer to them when doing the Exercises and Real Session later in the unit.

④**Exercise 1**   Practice for accustoming yourself to the sounds of the Japanese language and understanding its meaning. The sentence patterns are simple and particular emphasis is placed on picking out vocabulary.

⑤**Exercise 2**   Practice forming and writing short sentences. The intent is for you to understand and retain important sentence patterns.

⑥**Short Interview**   Experience real communication by asking questions. You will make two or so questions and ask them to three people. Native Japanese speakers (your friends, host family, etc.) are ideal speaking partners, but you can ask classmates if you must. Try as much as you can to keep the conversations longer than one question and answer.

⑦**Preparation & Rehearsal**   Preparation for the Real Session. Use what you studied in the unit and, working alone or in groups, prepare conversation topics, manuscripts, tools and so on. In addition, by determining the direction of the conversation and practicing with classmates, you will be able to interact with visitors confidently and smoothly.

⑧**Real Session**   A real communication activity with native Japanese-speaking visitors. This is the compilation of what you have studied in the unit and all of your studies thus far. If you have come this far, then you should have learned the required items (vocabulary and expressions) and conversational tricks, and you should be accustomed to communicating in this setting. So during the real thing, do not worry about mistakes and do not hesitate about communicating.

⑨**KAIWA master!**   An introduction to conversational tricks that are helpful for communication.

Sometimes you can dramatically expand a conversation with just a few words, such as asking a question in return, empathetic listening, asking additional questions and using trailing/incomplete sentences. Do not hesitate to use the advice written here.

⑩**Notes** An introduction to sociolinguistic and sociocultural information that is helpful for communication. This section covers topics such as the informal style and end-of-sentence particles. When you understand the appropriate settings for using them and their functions, they will help you during real communication.

⑪**Extra Lesson** Three small lessons between units. Study them if you find them interesting.

Other Study Content

· **Distinctive Features of the Japanese Language** At the end of the book is a summary of the distinctive linguistic features of Japanese. Refer to this section as needed. It will help you obtain a more systematic understanding of the language.

· **[Supplement] Vocabulary List** Lists of vocabulary appearing in each unit and categorized vocabulary lists that may help in the Real Sessions and in everyday life in Japan. Remove it from the book and use it as you see fit.

The People in This Book

Chris
(An exchange student from the U.S.)　Chris's friends　Chris's classmates　Chris's teacher　Chris's host family

本教材について（お使いになる先生方へ）

　本教材は、日本語を学習するビギナー向けの会話中心の総合教材です。ビギナーであっても周りの人とのコミュニケーションを楽しめるように、必要な日本語が効率的に習得できるよう作られています。各ユニットの最後には日本人との活動が組み込まれており、授業の中で実際のコミュニケーションを体験させることを目標としています。数週間から３か月までの短期留学生を主な対象としていますが、中長期の交換留学生のクラスや、海外での留学前クラスでも役立てていただけると思います。

　また、本教材はJ.V.ネウストプニー氏による「インターアクションのための日本語教育」の考え方に基づいています。インターアクションができるようになるためには、語彙や文型などの「言語能力」だけではなく、相手や場面に適した言語使用のための「社会言語能力」や、社会の中で自らの行動を理解するための「社会文化能力」も必要とされています。教師は、学習者がこれらのことに意識を向けるよう促すこと、およびそのために実際に日本人とコミュニケーションをする機会を提供することが期待されます。

Ⅰ．本教材の特長

①「初対面」から「帰国」まで、留学生が遭遇する場面を軸に6つのユニットで構成

　ビギナーが限られた留学期間において、「いつか上手になる」ためにではなく、「今日からコミュニケーションに参加できる」ように場面を選び、構成しました。特に短期留学生は、必要なことを効率よく学習することで、短い留学期間をより有益に過ごせるようになります。

②初期段階から会話ストラテジーや普通体の会話を学習

　聞き返し、あいづち、質問など、周りの人と積極的にコミュニケーションを図れるような会話ストラテジーの学習を初期段階から取り入れています。また、友人など身近な人との人間関係を意識し、普通体の会話も最初から学習します。これにより、ビギナーであっても受身一方ではなく、主体的に会話が進められ、自己表現を通じて人的ネットワークを築くことができます。

③授業の中で日本人との実際のコミュニケーションを体験

　ビギナーが教室外で実際のコミュニケーションを自ら行うことには困難や恐怖が伴いがちです。本教材は、授業活動として母語話者との実際のコミュニケーションが体験できるようになっています。事前に教室で学習した知識を使って準備をし、十分な練習をして実際の活動に臨むことで、困難を克服しつつ小さい成功体験を積み重ねながら自信をつけることができます。

　さらに、授業内でコミュニケーションができたという経験は、クラス外のコミュニケーションへの動機となり、自分で実際にやってみることにつながります。

④学習者にとっての有用性と負担のバランスが考慮された学習項目

　文型・語彙・表現等の学習項目は、ビギナーにとって必要性が高い項目、多くの場面で使える汎用性が高い項目、自己表現に必要な項目などを中心に、学習者にとっての有用性を考えて厳選されています。また、必要なときには学習者が自ら参照し、体系的に整理できるよう、日本語の言語的特徴や索引をまとめてあります。

Ⅱ．各ユニットの構成と流れ

　1ユニットの授業時間は、Real Sessionを含めて10〜12時間程度を想定しています。それぞれの機関、コースに合わせてお使いください。

①Goals　ユニットの目標を確認します。また、ここで最後のReal Sessionの内容を確認すると、目標とするコミュニケーションのイメージをつかむことができ、学習へのモチベーションが高まります。各ユニットの最後のcheckと対応しているので、学生の振り返りの目安ともなります。

②Short Dialogues　イラストや訳を見ながら場面のイメージをつかみます。音声を聞きながら理解して言ってみます。Unit 1の自己紹介などは、できれば自分のことに置きかえるのがよいでしょう。必要に応じて次のExpressionsを参照します。スマイルのマークは友だちや家族など、身近な人と話すときに使われる表現を表します。

③Expressions　Short Dialoguesの理解に必要であれば参照します。すべてを網羅的に学習する必要はありません。ExerciseやReal Sessionで学習者が必要になったときに各自で参照することもできます。

Advancedの項目は、ややレベルが上がりますが学習者からの発話の希望が多い項目です。使いたい学習者が各自で使うようにするのがよいでしょう。Short DialoguesやExerciseには出てこないので省略しても授業の進行に影響がありません。

④**Exercise 1**　日本語の音に慣れ、聴いて意味を理解する練習です。語彙の聞き取りに重点を置いており、文型は単純です。内容が把握できれば十分で、一言一句厳密に聞き取る必要はありません。練習の前に、関連する語彙を別冊の語彙リストで確認しておくとよいでしょう。

⑤**Exercise 2**　文型を意識しながら、短文を完成したり、質問に答える練習です。本教材では、文型に焦点をあてる練習はこれだけです。文法を体系的に理解したい学習者は、この練習を通して、Expressionsや巻末の文法の説明を参照しながら理解に努めるとよいでしょう。

⑥**Small Interview**　2つ程度の質問を作って3人の人に聞きます。相手はできれば母語話者（友人、ホストファミリーなど）が望ましいですが、クラスメイトでもかまいません。できるだけ、一問一答で終わらずに、会話の続け方の例を見て会話が続くようにします。事前にKAIWA master!で聞き返しやあいづちの練習をしておくとよいでしょう。ここは、短いながらも実際のコミュニケーションの練習です。細かい間違いはあまり気にせず、コミュニケーションを達成することを目標にします。

⑦**Preparation & Rehearsal**　ユニットで学習したことを使って、グループあるいは個人でReal Sessionの準備をします。個人作業になる場合も、できるだけクラスメイトと協力しながら楽しく行うことが、学び合いの観点からも望ましいです。自分が表現したいことや学習成果を最大限に発揮できるよう、よく準備します。

　　Real Sessionの具体的なイメージをつかんでから、クラスメイトと一度練習します。本番では、必ずしも予想通りの展開にはなりませんが、ある程度予想を立てて練習しておくと、緊張せずに、スムーズに対応することができます。

⑧**Real Session**　ユニットで学習したこと、および今までの学習の集大成です。学習者にとってはハレの日です。これまでの学習の流れで、コミュニケーションへの慣れができているはずですから、本番では、間違いを気にせず、積極的に話をさせます。学習者自身も、来てくれたビジターの方も楽しめるようなリラックスした雰囲気を作りましょう。はじめのうちは学習者は緊張します。教師やビジターが細かい間違いを指摘したり、段取り通りに進めることに神経質になりすぎて、会話の流れを阻害したり、学習者が母語話者と話すのを怖がってしまったりすることがないように注意しましょう。ビジターにも、活動の趣旨や流れをあらかじめ伝えて、学習者の日本語を直したり、言い直させたりするのではなく、内容重視のコミュニケーションをしてもらえるように伝えておくといいでしょう。

　　ビジターは、学習者3人にビジター1人、あるいは学習者とビジターが同数ぐらいが理想ですが、難しい場合はクラス全体に1人でもかまいません。ビジターが1人いる場合とまったくいない場合では、活動の意義が大きく異なります。地域の国際交流協会に登録しているボランティアの方、近隣に居住されている方、あるいは、同じ学校や近所の学校の日本人学生、学校の職員の方など、誰でもビジターとして活動できます。

⑨**KAIWA master!**　聞き返し、あいづち、質問、言いさしなど、コミュニケーションを主体的に、かつ

円滑に進めるための会話ストラテジーを各ユニットで紹介しています。そのユニットに特に関連があることを扱っていますが、どの内容も普段の会話に役立つことなので、先取りすることも可能です。文法的に正しい完全な文が作れるようになってから会話を学習し始めるのではなく、学習の初期段階から、相手とのやりとりの中で、相手に助けられながらコミュニケーションを進めていくことを実感できるようにしています。

⑩**Notes**　コミュニケーションに役立つ社会言語的、社会文化的な情報を紹介しています。普通体や終助詞などは、形式を完全に習得しなくても、使う場面や機能を理解して、少しずつ使えるようになればいいものと位置づけ、学習項目ではなくNotesで紹介しています。各ユニットに関連があることを扱っていますが、どれも常に役に立つ内容なので先取りして学習することが可能です。

⑪**Extra Lesson**　ユニットの間に、小さいレッスンが３つあります。会話を楽しみながら、日常生活ですぐに使う語彙・表現を学びます。新しい文型も含まれていますが、文型としてではなく、ここでは表現としてまるごと学習します。学習者が文型に興味を持った場合は、簡単に説明し練習してもかまいません。

巻末には、日本語の言語としての特徴がまとめられています。必要に応じて参照するようにしてください。体系的な知識の獲得に役立ちます。

また、別冊として、各ユニットに出てくる語彙のリスト、Real Sessionや日常生活に役立ちそうなカテゴリー別語彙リスト、よく使う動詞の活用表があります。

この本のローマ字表記は、ヘボン式を基本としていますが、いくつかの例外があります。

・長音は、母音の上に横棒をつけて表します。例：Tōkyō
・「映画」や「ええ」などはかな表記に合わせてeiga、eeとしています。
・い形容詞の語尾は活用変化を考えてiとしています。例：oishii
・接辞はハイフンで区切っている場合があります。例：Kurisu-san

教材作成にあたって

　本教材は、著者らが神田外語大学留学生別科の「実践日本語Ⅰ」を担当しつつ開発してきた教材が基になっています。授業の段階からいろいろとアドバイスをくださった先生方、多くのフィードバックを提供してくれた交換留学生およびIES東京センターの留学生の皆さんに感謝いたします。

Contents

おはようございます。
Ohayō gozaimasu.
Good morning.

おはよう。
Ohayō.
Good morning.

こんにちは。
Konnichiwa.
Hello.

こんばんは。
Konbanwa.
Good evening.

さようなら。*
Sayōnara.
Good bye.

じゃあまた（ね）。
またね。
Jāmata（ne）. / Matane.
Bye bye.

＊Not used much outside of school. Sounds like a permanent farewell.

（どうも）ありがとう。
（Dōmo）arigatō.
Thank you.

（どうも）ありがとうございます。
（Dōmo）arigatō gozaimasu.
Thank you.

いいえ。
Iie.
You're welcome.

すみません。
Sumimasen.
Sorry.

いいえ。
Iie.
Never mind.

すみません。
Sumimasen.
Thank you.

いいえ。
Iie.
You're welcome.

いただきます。
Itadakimasu.
Let's eat.

ごちそうさまでした。
Gochisōsama deshita.
Thank you for the meal.

いってきます。
Ittekimasu.
I'll be back.

いってらっしゃい。
Itterasshai.
See you later.

ただいま。
Tadaima.
I'm back.

おかえりなさい。
Okaerinasai.
Welcome back.

おやすみなさい。
Oyasuminasai
Good night.

すみません。
Sumimasen.
Excuse me.

これ、何ですか。
Kore, nan desu ka.
What is this?

トイレ、どこですか。
Toire, doko desu ka.
Where is the bathroom?

これ、お願いします。
Kore, onegaishimasu.
This one please.

はい。／ええ。
Hai. / Ee.   Yes.

いいえ。
Iie.   No.

大丈夫ですか。
Daijōbu desu ka.
Are you alright?

はい、大丈夫です。
Hai, daijōbu desu.
I'm alright.

わかります。
Wakarimasu.
I understand.

わかりません。
Wakarimasen.
I don't understand.

もう一度／ゆっくり、お願いします。
Mō ichido / yukkuri, onegaishimasu.
Could you say that again/more slowly?

×××は英語／日本語で何ですか。
xxx wa Eigo/Nihon-go de nan desu ka.
How do you say xxx in English/Japanese?

聞いてください。
Kiite kudasai.
Please listen.

見てください。
Mite kudasai.
Please take a look.

Making Friends
—よろしくお願いします—

Goals

1. Introduce yourself to a person you have met for the first time.

2. Ask a person you have met for the first time some questions, such as what his/her name is, where he/she is from, and what his/her interests are.

3. Continue the conversation as you expand the topics and ask questions back.

〈At a party〉

こんにちは。えみです。
Konnichiwa. Emi desu.
Hello. I'm Emi.

はじめまして。
Hajimemashite.
Nice to meet you.

あのー、お名前は？
Anō, o-namae wa?
Um, what's your name?

クリスです。はじめまして。
Kurisu desu. Hajimemashite.
I'm Chris. Nice to meet you.

アメリカから来ました。
Amerika kara kimashita.
I'm from the U.S.

よろしくお願いします。
Yoroshiku onegaishimasu.
I hope we can be friends.

よろしくお願いします。
Yoroshiku onegaishimasu.
Me, too.

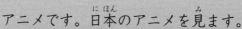

 クリスさん、しゅみは何ですか。 Chris, what kind of things do you like?
Kurisu-san, Shumi wa nan desu ka.

アニメです。日本のアニメを見ます。
Anime desu. Nihon no anime o mimasu.
I'm into cartoons. I watch Japanese cartoons（anime）.

そうですか。 Is that so?
Sō desu ka.

えみさんは音楽が好きですか。
Emi-san wa ongaku ga suki desu ka?
Do you like music?

はい、好きです。よく音楽を聞きます。クリスさんは？
Hai, suki desu. Yoku ongaku o kikimasu. Kurisu-san wa?
Yes I do. I often listen to music. How about you?

私も好きです。　　　　I like music, too.
Watashi mo suki desu.

⟨At the end of the party⟩

これ、私のメールアドレス。
Kore, watashi no mēru adoresu.
This is my e-mail address.

ありがとう。メールする。
Arigatō. Mēru suru.
Thanks. I'll e-mail you.

じゃあ、また。
Jā, mata.
Good bye.

うん。じゃあ、またね。
Un. Jā, matane.
See you again.

Expressions

Noun sentence

（私は）学生です。
(Watashi wa) gakusei desu.

I'm a student.

（私は）学生じゃないです。
(Watashi wa) gakusei janai desu.

I'm not a student.

学生ですか。
Gakusei desu ka.

Are you a student?

はい、学生です。／
はい、そうです。
Hai, gakusei desu./
Hai, sō desu.

Yes, I am.

いいえ、学生じゃないです。／
いいえ、ちがいます。
Iie, gakusei janai desu./
Iie, chigaimasu.

No, I'm not.

Verb sentence

（私は）映画を見ます。*
(Watashi wa) eiga o mimasu.

I watch movies.

（私は）映画を見ません。
(Watashi wa) eiga o mimasen.

I don't watch movies.

（私は）きのう映画を
見ました。
(Watashi wa) kinō eiga o mimashita.

I watched a movie yesterday.

（私は）きのう映画を
見ませんでした。
(Watashi wa) kinō eiga o mimasen deshita.

I didn't watch a movie yesterday.

＊The nonpast form is also used to express future events.

（私は）あした映画を見ます。
(Watashi wa) ashita eiga o mimasu.

I'll watch a movie tomorrow.

14

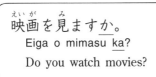

映画を見ますか。
Eiga o mimasu ka?
Do you watch movies?

はい、見ます。 Yes, I do.
Hai, mimasu.

いいえ、見ません。 No, I don't.
Iie, mimasen.

Noun + が好きです Noun + ga suki desu

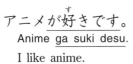

アニメが好きです。
Anime ga suki desu.
I like anime.

アニメが好きじゃないです。
Anime ga suki janai desu.
I don't like anime.

Particles

私はクリスです。 Watashi wa Kurisu desu.	I'm Chris.
（私は）アニメを見ます。 (Watashi wa) anime o mimasu.	I watch anime.
（私は）アメリカから来ました。 (Watashi wa) Amerika kara kimashita.	I came from the U.S.
（私は）アニメが好きです。 (Watashi wa) anime ga suki desu.	I like anime.
私も（アニメが）好きです。 Watashi mo (anime ga) suki desu.	I like anime, too.
（私は）渋谷に／へ行きます。 (Watashi wa) Shibuya ni/e ikimasu.	I go to Shibuya.
（私は）渋谷で買い物をします。 (Watashi wa) Shibuya de kaimono o shimasu.	I go shopping in Shibuya.
日本の音楽／私のメールアドレス Nihon no ongaku / Watashi no mēru adoresu.	Japanese music / My e-mail address.
アニメと音楽 Anime to ongaku	Anime and music

Question words

何／何　*nan/nani* (what)

A：しゅみは何ですか。
Shumi wa <u>nan</u> desu ka.
What kind of things do you like?

B：アニメです。
Anime desu.
I like anime.

A：何が好きですか。
<u>Nani</u> ga suki desu ka.
What do you like?

B：アニメが好きです。
Anime ga suki desu.
I like anime.

どこ　*doko* (where)

A：どこから来ましたか。
<u>Doko</u> kara kimashita ka.
Where did you come from?

B：アメリカから来ました。
Amerika kara kimashita.
I came from the U.S.

A：しゅっしんはどこですか。
Shusshin wa <u>doko</u> desu ka.
Where are you from?

B：アメリカです。
Amerika desu.
I'm from the U.S.

だれ　*dare* (who)

A：だれが好きですか。
<u>Dare</u> ga suki desu ka.

B：ジョニー・デップが好きです。
Jonī Deppu ga suki desu.

Who do you like?

I like Johnny Depp.

どうして／なんで　*dōshite/nande* (why)

A：どうして／なんで 日本語を勉強しますか。
<u>Dōshite/nande</u> Nihon-go o benkyō shimasu ka.

Why do you study Japanese?

B：私は日本のアニメが好きです。
Watashi wa Nihon no anime ga suki desu.

I like Japanese anime.

どんな　*donna* (what kind of)

A：どんな音楽が好きですか。
<u>Donna</u> ongaku ga suki desu ka.

What kind of music do you like?

B：Jポップが好きです。
J-poppu ga suki desu.

I like J-pop.

Adverbs of frequency

毎日
まいにち
mainichi　everyday

よく
yoku　often

ときどき
tokidoki　sometimes

本を読みます
ほん　よ
hon o yomimasu
I read books

あまり
amari　(not)often

ぜんぜん
zenzen　never
(not)at all

本を読みません
ほん　よ
hon o yomimasen
I don't read books

Supportive responses

そうですか。　　Is that so?
Sō desu ka.

▶ See p.50 KAIWA master!

Noun ＋ は？　Noun ＋ wa?

クリスさんは？　　And you?
Kurisu-san wa?

▶ See p.23 KAIWA master!

Advanced

Noun ＋ に住んでいます　Noun ＋ ni sunde'imasu
す

A：どこに住んでいますか。　Where do you live?
　　す
　　Doko ni sunde'imasu ka.

B：東京に住んでいます。　I live in Tokyo.
　　とうきょう　す
　　Tōkyō ni sunde'imasu.

Verb ＋ こと　Verb ＋ koto

本を読むことが好きです。　I like reading books.
ほん　よ　　　　　す
Hon o yomu koto ga suki desu.

しゅみは音楽を聞くことです。　I enjoy listening to music.
　　　　おんがく　き
Shumi wa ongaku o kiku koto desu.

▶ See p.104 for the dictionary form

You can use informal expressions when speaking with people close to you, such as your family and friends.

すしが好きですか。
Sushi ga suki desu ka.

すし、好き？
Sushi, suki?

Do you like sushi?

はい、好きです。
Hai, suki desu.

うん、好き。
Un, suki.

Yes, I do.

いいえ、好きじゃないです。
Iie, suki janai desu.

ううん、好きじゃない。
Uun, suki janai.

No, I don't.

すしを食べますか。
Sushi o tabemasu ka.

すし、食べる？
Sushi, taberu?

Do you eat sushi?

はい、食べます。
Hai, tabemasu.

うん、食べる。
Un, taberu.

Yes, I do.

いいえ、食べません。
Iie, tabemasen.

ううん、食べない。
Uun, tabenai.

No, I don't.

きのう、渋谷に
行きましたか。
Kinō, Shibuya ni ikimashita ka.

きのう、渋谷に
行った？
Kinō, Shibuya ni itta?

Did you go to Shibuya yesterday?

はい、行きました。
Hai, ikimashita.

うん、行った。
Un, itta.

Yes, I did.

いいえ、行きませんでした。
Iie, ikimasen deshita.

ううん、行かなかった。
Uun, ikanakatta.

No, I didn't.

▶ See p.98 for the details

▶ CD track 06

See the vocabulary list for Unit 1. Listen to the self-introductions, and then complete the table below.

	Name	I'm from...	Occupation	Other information
Ex.	クリス Kurisu	アメリカ Amerika	大学生 Daigakusei	アニメが好きです。 Anime ga suki desu.
1.	シン Shin			
2.	カルロス Karurosu			
3.	アート Āto			

Exercise 2

Write about yourself using words such as those given in the example. Share the sentences you make with your classmates.

Ex. 毎日コーヒーを飲みます。
    Mainichi kōhī o nomimasu.

1. (私は) 毎日
    (Watashi wa) mainichi
_____

2. (私は) ときどき
    (Watashi wa) tokidoki
_____

3. (私は) あまり
    (Watashi wa) amari
_____

4. (私は) きのう
    (Watashi wa) kinō
_____

5. (私は) あした
    (Watashi wa) ashita
_____

Ask three people about their hobbies. Try to keep the conversation going as long as possible.

Ex.　A：しゅみは何ですか。　　　　　　　　What kind of things do you like?
　　　　Shumi wa nan desu ka.

　　　B：スポーツです。　　　　　　　　　　It's sports.
　　　　Supōtsu desu.

　　　A：どんなスポーツが好きですか。　　　　What sport do you like?
　　　　Donna supōtsu ga suki desu ka.

　　　B：サッカーが好きです。　　　　　　　I like soccer.
　　　　Sakkā ga suki desu.

　　　A：そうですか。よくサッカーをしますか。　Nice. Do you play often?
　　　　Sō desu ka. Yoku sakkā o shimasu ka.

Name	Answer

Notes　"あなた anata"

　The word "あなた *anata*" (you) is seldom used in conversation. In certain situations, the use of this word might sound slightly cold or impolite to the person with whom you are speaking. To avoid sounding distant, call the other person by his/her name or title, such as "せんせい *sensei*" (teacher, doctor). If the context is clear, you can omit all the words that correspond to "you".

Ex.　~~あなたの~~しゅみは何ですか。　　What kind of things do you like?
　　　~~Anata no~~ shumi wa nan desu ka.

（えみさんの）
しゅみは何ですか。

20

1. Read Chris's example, and then write about yourself.

こんにちは。クリスです。アメリカから来ました。
大学生（だいがくせい）です。

Konnichiwa. Kurisu desu. Amerika kara kimashita.
Daigakusei desu.

Hello. I'm Chris. I'm from the U.S. I'm a university student.

しゅみはアニメです。日本（にほん）のアニメが好（す）きです。
音楽（おんがく）も好（す）きです。ギターをひきます。

Shumi wa anime desu. Nihon no anime ga suki desu.
Ongaku mo suki desu. Gitā o hikimasu.

I'm into cartoons. I like Japanese cartoons (anime). I also like
music. I play the guitar.

よろしくお願（ねが）いします。

Yoroshiku onegaishimasu.

I hope we can be friends.

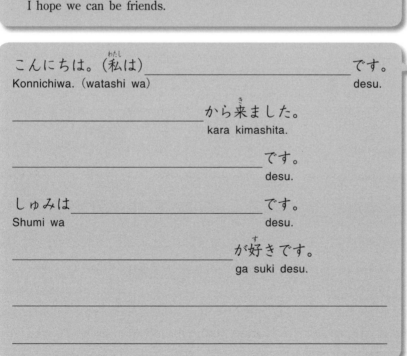

こんにちは。（私（わたし）は）＿＿＿＿＿＿＿＿＿＿＿＿＿＿です。
Konnichiwa. (watashi wa)   desu.

＿＿＿＿＿＿＿＿＿＿から来（き）ました。
                    kara kimashita.

＿＿＿＿＿＿＿＿＿＿＿＿＿＿です。
                              desu.

しゅみは＿＿＿＿＿＿＿＿＿＿＿です。
Shumi wa   desu.

＿＿＿＿＿＿＿＿＿＿＿が好（す）きです。
                    ga suki desu.

＿＿＿＿＿＿＿＿＿＿＿＿＿＿＿＿＿＿＿＿

＿＿＿＿＿＿＿＿＿＿＿＿＿＿＿＿＿＿＿＿

2. Practice with a classmate as you look at the Short Dialogues on p.12-13. Talk about yourself
   and ask questions about your partner.

Real Session

友<ruby>とも</ruby>だちを作<ruby>つく</ruby>ろう！　Make some friends!

Have fun speaking with people you meet for the first time. Use what you have learned in this unit and try to keep the conversation going as long as you can.

> 1. Make small groups, including visitors.

> 2. Each person will make a self-introduction.

> 3. Have an enjoyable conversation with the visitors about hobbies, what you like and so forth.

> 4. If you think you want to meet a visitor again, exchange contact info.

--- **check** --

1. Introduce yourself to a person you have met for the first time.
   かんぺき　No problem □　　だいじょうぶ　OK □　　まだ　Not yet □

2. Ask a person you have met for the first time some questions, such as what his/her name is, where he/she is from, and what his/her interests are.
   かんぺき　No problem □　　だいじょうぶ　OK □　　まだ　Not yet □

3. Continue the conversation as you expand the topics and ask questions back.
   かんぺき　No problem □　　だいじょうぶ　OK □　　まだ　Not yet □

If you don't understand what someone said, use one of the following expressions.
When speaking with friends, a simple "え? *e?*" is enough.

- すみません。もう一度お願いします。   Sorry. Please say that again.
 Sumimasen. Mō ichido onegaishimasu.

- すみません。ゆっくりお願いします。   Sorry. Please speak more slowly.
 Sumimasen. Yukkuri onegaishimasu.

- 〜は何ですか。   What is 〜?
 〜wa nan desu ka.

 Ex. A：私のしゅみは料理です。   I enjoy *ryōri*.
        Watashi no shumi wa ryōri desu.

 B：「りょうり」は 何ですか。   What's "*ryōri*"?
        "Ryōri" wa nan desu ka.

 A："Cooking"です。   It's the word for "cooking".
        "Cooking" desu.

You can use these simple expressions to expand the conversation.

☺ 私も！   Me, too! / Me, neither!
 Watashi mo!

 えみさんは？   How about you? / How about Emi?
 Emi-san wa?

▶See p.20 Notes

Unit 2

Going out to Eat
―サンドイッチ、お願^{ねが}いします―

Goals

1. Answer questions from restaurant staff.

2. Order a meal.

3. Pay your bill at a restaurant.

⟨At a restaurant⟩

Restaurant staff use very polite Japanese. You do not have to use it, but it would be better if you can understand it.

いらっしゃいませ。何名様ですか。
Irasshaimase. Nan-mei-sama desu ka.
Welcome. How many people?

2人です。　Two.
Futari desu.

おたばこは？　Smoking or non-smoking?
O-tabako wa ?

きんえんで／きつえんで。　Non-smoking. / Smoking.
Kin'en de / kitsuen de.

どうぞ、こちらへ。　This way, please.
Dōzo, kochira e.

⟨At the table⟩

ご注文は？　Shall I take your order?
Go-chūmon wa?

サンドイッチ、お願いします。　A sandwich, please.
Sandoicchi, onegaishimasu.

私はハンバーグ定食。　I'll have the Hamburg steak set.
Watashi wa hanbāgu teishoku.

お飲み物は？　And your drinks?
O-nomimono wa?

あとで、コーヒー2つ、ください。
Atode, kōhī futatsu, kudasai.
Two coffees, but after our meal.

かしこまりました。少々お待ちください。
Kashikomarimashita. Shōshō omachi kudasai.
Sure. Just a moment, please.

〈After the meal〉

あのー、すみません。コーヒー、まだでしょうか。
Anō, sumimasen. Kōhī, mada deshō ka.
Um, excuse me. Are the coffees not ready yet?

もうしわけありません。すぐにお持ちします。
Mōshiwake arimasen. Suguni omochi shimasu.
I'm so sorry. I'll bring them right away.

〈At the cash register〉

お願いします。　Check, please.
Onegaishimasu.

ごいっしょですか。　Together?
Goissho desu ka.

いえ、べつべつにお願いします。私はハンバーグ定食と
コーヒー。

Ie, betsubetsu ni onegaishimasu. Watashi wa hanbāgu teishoku to kōhī.

No, separately, please. I had the Hamburg steak set and a coffee.

1,000円です。   That'll be 1,000 yen.
Sen-en desu.

ごちそうさまでした。   Thank you very much.
Gochisōsama deshita.

ありがとうございました。
Arigatō gozaimashita.

And thank you!

〈At a fast-food restaurant〉

いらっしゃいませ。こちらでおめしあがりですか。
お持ち帰りですか。

Irasshaimase. Kochira de omeshiagari desu ka. Omochikaeri
desu ka.

Welcome. Here or to-go?

持ち帰りです。ハンバーガーのM、1つお願いします。
Mochikaeri desu. Hanbāgā no emu, hitotsu onegaishimasu.

To-go. One medium hamburger, please.

Expressions

Ordering something

サンドイッチ、お願いします。 Sandoicchi, onegaishimasu.	A sandwich, please.
コーヒー2つ、ください。 Kōhī futatsu, kudasai.	Two coffees, please.

"お願いします onegaishimasu" is a handy expression that you can also use when you request something from a person.

〈At the cash register〉お願いします。 Onegaishimasu.	Check, please.
べつべつにお願いします。 Betsubetsu ni onegaishimasu.	Separately, please.

Verbs for existence

メニュー、ありますか。 Menyū, arimasu ka. Do you have a menu?	英語のメニュー、ありますか。 Eigo no menyū, arimasu ka. Do you have an English menu?
customer：トイレはどこにありますか。 Toire wa doko ni arimasu ka.	Where is the restroom?
waiter ：こちらです。どうぞ。 Kochira desu. Dōzo.	This way, please.

Use "います imasu" for people and animals.

クリスさんはどこにいますか。 Kurisu-san wa doko ni imasu ka.	Where is Chris?

Adverbs for quantity

お酒を　　⎡ たくさん／いっぱい*　⎤ 飲みました。
Osake o (alcohol) ⎢ takusan/ippai (a lot) ⎢ nomimashita (drank)
　　　　　⎢ 少し／ちょっと* 　　　⎥ * "いっぱい *ippai*" and "ちょっと
　　　　　⎣ sukoshi/chotto (a little) ⎦ chotto" are casual expressions.

Numbers and counters

0	れい（ぜろ） rei (zero)

	Things	People
1	ひと 1つ hitotsu	ひとり 1人 hitori
2	ふた 2つ futatsu	ふたり 2人 futari
3	みっ 3つ mittsu	さんにん 3人 san-nin
4	よっ 4つ yottsu	よにん 4人 yo-nin
5	いつ 5つ itsutsu	ごにん 5人 go-nin
6	むっ 6つ muttsu	ろくにん 6人 roku-nin
7	なな 7つ nanatsu	しちにん 7人 shichi-nin
8	やっ 8つ yattsu	はちにん 8人 hachi-nin
9	ここの 9つ kokonotsu	きゅうにん 9人 kyū-nin
10	とお 10 tō	じゅうにん 10人 jū-nin

Numbers 1–10 (left column):

1	いち ichi
2	に ni
3	さん san
4	し（よん） shi (yon)
5	ご go
6	ろく roku
7	しち（なな） shichi (nana)
8	はち hachi
9	きゅう（く） kyū (ku)
10	じゅう jū

Ex.

なんめいさま

コーヒー2つ、お願いします。
Kōhi futatsu, onegaishimasu.
Two coffees, please.

A：何名様ですか。
Nan-mei-sama desu ka.
How many people?

B：5人です。
Go-nin desu.
Five.

10	じゅう jū	100	ひゃく hyaku	1,000	（いっ）せん sen / issen	10,000	いちまん ichiman
20	にじゅう nijū	200	にひゃく nihyaku	2,000	にせん nisen	20,000	にまん niman
30	さんじゅう sanjū	300	さんびゃく sanbyaku	3,000	さんぜん sanzen	30,000	さんまん sanman
40	よんじゅう yonjū	400	よんひゃく yonhyaku	4,000	よんせん yonsen	40,000	よんまん yonman
50	ごじゅう gojū	500	ごひゃく gohyaku	5,000	ごせん gosen	50,000	ごまん goman
60	ろくじゅう rokujū	600	ろっぴゃく roppyaku	6,000	ろくせん rokusen	60,000	ろくまん rokuman
70	ななじゅう nanajū	700	ななひゃく nanahyaku	7,000	ななせん nanasen	70,000	ななまん nanaman
80	はちじゅう hachijū	800	はっぴゃく happyaku	8,000	はっせん hassen	80,000	はちまん hachiman
90	きゅうじゅう kyūjū	900	きゅうひゃく kyūhyaku	9,000	きゅうせん kyūsen	90,000	きゅうまん kyūman
						100,000	じゅうまん jūman

Ex.

38 さんじゅう はち
sanjū hachi

69 ろくじゅう きゅう
rokujū kyū

245 にひゃく よんじゅう ご
nihyaku yonjū go

624 ろっぴゃく にじゅう よん
roppyaku nijū yon

1,711 <u>せん</u> ななひゃく じゅう いち
sen nanahyaku jū ichi

8,872 はっせん はっぴゃく ななじゅう に
hassen happyaku nanajū ni

43,157 よんまん さんぜん ひゃく ごじゅう なな
yonman sanzen hyaku gojū nana

71,343 ななまん <u>いっせん</u> さんびゃく よんじゅう さん
nanaman issen sanbyaku yonjū san

Question words

いくら *ikura* (how much)

A：<u>いくら</u>ですか。
　　Ikura desu ka.

B：300 円です。
　　Sanbyaku-en desu.

How much is it?

300 yen.

いくつ *ikutsu* (how many)

A：<u>いくつ</u>ですか。
　　Ikutsu desu ka.

B：2つお願いします。
　　Futatsu onegaishimasu.

How many?

Two, please.

何人 *nan-nin* (how many people)

A：今日のパーティー、<u>何人</u>来ますか。
　　Kyō no pāthī, <u>nan-nin</u> kimasu ka.

B：10人来ます。
　　Jū-nin kimasu.

How many people are coming to the party today?

Ten people will come.

どう *dō* (how)

A：日本料理は<u>どう</u>ですか。
　　Nihon-ryōri wa <u>dō</u> desu ka.

B：おいしいです。
　　Oishii desu.

How do you like Japanese food?

It's delicious.

Exercise 1 ▶ **CD track 09, 10, 11**

Listen to the Japanese and write down numbers and prices.

Ⅰ. How many people?

Ex. ___3___ 1. _____ 2. _____ 3. _____

4. _____ 5. _____ 6. _____

Ⅱ. How many?

Ex. ___2___ 1. _____ 2. _____ 3. _____

4. _____ 5. _____ 6. _____

Ⅲ. How much?

Ex. 1. 2. 3. 4.

___150___ 円 _{えん} en _____ 円 _{えん} en _____ 円 _{えん} en _____ 円 _{えん} en _____ 円 _{えん} en

5. 6. 7. Listen to the question and answer it.

_____ 円 _{えん} en _____ 円 _{えん} en _____ 円 _{えん} en

Exercise 2

Answer the questions, and then share the sentences you make with your classmates.

Ex. きのう、どこに行きましたか。　　　　Where did you go yesterday?
Kinō, doko ni ikimashita ka.

　レストランに行きました。　Resutoran ni ikimashita.

1. きのう、何を食べましたか。　　　　What did you eat yesterday?
Kinō, nani o tabemashita ka.

2. 日本料理が好きですか。何が好きですか。 Do you like Japanese food? What do you like?
   Nihon-ryōri ga suki desu ka. Nani ga suki desu ka.

---

3. 日本料理はどうですか。 How do you like Japanese food?
   Nihon-ryōri wa dō desu ka.

---

4. どこで昼ご飯を食べますか。 Where do you eat lunch?
   Doko de hirugohan o tabemasu ka.

---

5. よくお酒を飲みますか。 Do you drink alcohol much?
   Yoku osake o nomimasu ka.

Short Interview

Ask three people about their favorite foods and drinks.

1. どこでよくご飯を食べますか。 Where do you often eat food?
   Doko de yoku gohan o tabemasu ka.

2. 日本の食べ物はどうですか。 How do you like Japanese food?
   Nihon no tabemono wa dō desu ka.

3. 何が好きですか。 What do you like?
   Nani ga suki desu ka.

名前	1の答え	2の答え	3の答え

You can continue the conversation by asking the location of the restaurant after the first question and asking "どうしてですか *dōshite desu ka*" after the third question.

1. Form groups and make a restaurant menu. Think about the following as you do so.

   - What kind of restaurant will it be?
   - What kind of menu will you make?
   - What are appropriate prices?
   - What food will you recommend?

   You need to prepare: construction paper, leaflets with pictures of food, markers, scissors, glue and anything else you need.

   * Japanese uses kanji, hiragana, katakana, the alphabet and other symbols. There are certain rules for using each. For more details, please look at the explanation on p.94.

2. In groups, use the menus you made to practice conversations between restaurant customers and staff. Please refer to the Short Dialogues on p.26-28. All group members will practice as both customers and staff. When you are a customer, try to ask about the food's ingredients ("ざいりょうは何ですか *Zairyō wa nan desu ka*"), make requests and complain.

▶ See p.36 KAIWA master!

Real Session

Are you ready?

レストランに行こう！　Let's go to a restaurant!

The visitors will pretend to be the staff working at your imaginary restaurant. Go to the restaurant and play the roles of customers. Before you start the session, provide the visitors with a simple explanation about the restaurant and menu.

> 1. Go to the restaurant the visitors have opened. Answer questions from the staff.

> 2. Look at the menu (made in groups) and order. Ask the staff questions and make requests.

> 3. Pay the bill.

It's also fun to switch up the roles and try a new session.

--- **check** --

1. Answer questions from restaurant staff.
   かんぺき　No problem ☐　　だいじょうぶ　OK ☐　　まだ　Not yet ☐
2. Order a meal.
   かんぺき　No problem ☐　　だいじょうぶ　OK ☐　　まだ　Not yet ☐
3. Pay your bill at a restaurant.
   かんぺき　No problem ☐　　だいじょうぶ　OK ☐　　まだ　Not yet ☐

K A I W A master! ▶CD track 12

Use the following expressions when you want to complain or make a request.

- When the spoon is dirty
  新しいスプーン、お願いします。   Can I have new spoon, please?
  Atarashii supūn, onegaishimasu.

  新しいスプーン、ありますか。   Do you have any new spoons?
  Atarashii supūn, arimasu ka.

- When you are brought the wrong food
  これ、ちがいます。   This is the wrong thing.
  Kore, chigaimasu.

You do not have to use a complete sentence to make a simple inquiry about something you do not understand.

- すみません、トイレはどこですか。   →   すみません、トイレは…。
  Sumimasen, toire wa doko desu ka.   Sumimasen, toire wa...
  Excuse me. Where is the restroom?

- メニューはありますか。   →   メニューは？
  Menyū wa arimasu ka.   Menyū wa ?
  Do you have a menu?

Extra Lesson 1 　Invitations to Friends

Dialogue 1 　▶CD track 13

A：来週、おまつりがありますよ。いっしょに行きませんか。

Raishū, o-matsuri ga arimasu yo. <u>Issho ni ikimasen ka.</u>

There's a festival next week. Do you wanna go with me?

B：いいですね。いつですか。

Iidesu ne. Itsu desu ka.　Sounds good. When is it?

A：20日と21日、土曜日と日曜日です。どちらがいいですか。

Hatsuka to nijūichi-nichi, doyōbi to nichiyōbi desu. <u>Dochira ga ii desu ka.</u>

The 20th and 21st, Saturday and Sunday. Which is good for you?

B：私はどちらでもいいですよ。

Watashi wa <u>dochira demo ii desu</u> yo.　Either one is fine with me.

A：じゃあ、20日の土曜日に。

Jā, hatsuka no doyōbi ni.　Well, let's do Saturday the 20th.

B：ええ。

Ee.　Okay.

▶ See Vocablary List, calendar

Dialogue 2 　▶CD track 14

A：ねこカフェ、知ってる？ 渋谷のねこカフェ、いっしょに行かない？

Neko-kafe, shitteru? Shibuya no neko-kafe, <u>issho ni ikanai?</u>

Have you heard of cat cafes? Do you wanna go to the cat cafe in Shibuya with me?

B：うん、行きたい！ いつ行く？

Un, ikitai! Itsu iku?　Yeah, I do! When will we go?

▶ See p.44 for "shitteru?"
▶ See p.59 for "V-tai"

A：あしたは？

Ashita wa?　How about tomorrow?

B：あー、あしたはテストだ。ほかの日はどう？

Ā, ashita wa tesuto da. Hoka no hi <u>wa dō?</u>

Oh, I have a test tomorrow. How about a different day?

A：じゃあ、来週の月曜日は？

Jā, raishū no getsuyōbi wa?　Well, how about Monday of next week?

B：うん。たぶん、大丈夫。

Un. Tabun, daijōbu.　Yeah, that might work.

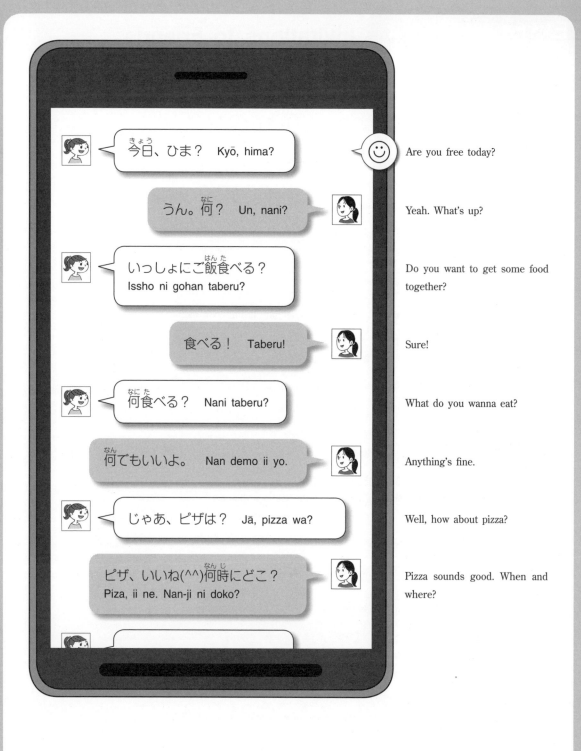

今日、ひま？ Kyō, hima?

Are you free today?

うん。何？ Un, nani?

Yeah. What's up?

いっしょにご飯食べる？
Issho ni gohan taberu?

Do you want to get some food together?

食べる！ Taberu!

Sure!

何食べる？ Nani taberu?

What do you wanna eat?

何でもいいよ。 Nan demo ii yo.

Anything's fine.

じゃあ、ピザは？ Jā, pizza wa?

Well, how about pizza?

ピザ、いいね(^^)何時にどこ？
Piza, ii ne. Nan-ji ni doko?

Pizza sounds good. When and where?

Unit 3

Asking Questions
―これは英語で何ですか―

Goals

1. Request something from a person.
2. Recommend something to a person.
3. Ask about things you do not understand and vocabulary.

〈At a library〉

すみません、ちょっと教えてください。
Sumimasen, chotto oshiete kudasai.
Excuse me. Can you tell me something?

はい。
Hai. Sure.

これは、英語で何ですか。
Kore wa, Eigo de nan desu ka.
What is this in English?

"search" ですよ。
"search" desu yo.
It's "search".

わかりました。どうもありがとうございます。
Wakarimashita. Dōmo arigatō gozaimasu.
I got it. Thank you very much.

このパソコンの使い方を知っていますか。
Kono pasokon no tsukai-kata o shitte'imasu ka.
Do you know how to use this computer?

はい。ここに本の名前を入れてください。
Hai. Koko ni hon no namae o irete kudasai.
Yes. Enter the name of a book here.

これでいいですか。
Kore de ii desu ka.
Is this OK?

〈At Chris's home〉

おじゃまします。
Ojamashimasu.
Excuse me.

どうぞ、すわってください。
Dōzo, suwatte kudasai.
Please, go ahead and take a seat.

サンドイッチを作りました。どうぞ、食べてください。
Sandoicchi o tsukurimashita. Dōzo, tabete kudasai.
I made sandwiches. Go ahead and eat.

V-てください   V-te kudasai

▶See p.105 for the te-form

ちょっと待ってください。
Chotto matte kudasai.

Please wait a moment.

どうぞ食べてください。
Dōzo tabete kudasai.

Please, go ahead and eat.

もう一度読んでください。
Mō ichido yonde kudasai.

Please read again.

どうぞすわってください。
Dōzo suwatte kudasai.

Please, go ahead and take a seat.

You can simply use "〜て 〜*te*" as an informal way to express "〜てください 〜*te kudasai*".

ちょっと待って。   Just a moment.
Chotto matte.

食べて、食べて。
Tabete, tabete.

Eat, eat.

すわって、すわって。
Suwatte, suwatte.

Sit, sit.

Demonstratives

これは何ですか。
Kore wa nan desu ka.

What's this?

それは何ですか。
Sore wa nan desu ka.

What' s that?

あれは何ですか。
Are wa nan desu ka.

What' s that over there?

えみさんのかばんはどれですか。
Emi-san no kaban wa <u>dore</u> desu ka.
Which one is Emi's bag?

この本を読みましたか。
Kono hon o yomimashita ka.

Have you read this book?

その本を読みましたか。
Sono hon o yomimashita ka.

Have you read that book?

あの本を読みましたか。
Ano hon o yomimashita ka.

Have you read that book over there?

どの本を読みましたか。
Dono hon o yomimashita ka.

Which book did you read?

	こ ko Near the speaker	そ so Near the listener	あ a Far from speaker/listener	ど do Question
thing	この + noun kono	その + noun sono	あの + noun ano	どの + noun dono
	これ kore	それ sore	あれ are	どれ dore
place	ここ koko	そこ soko	あそこ asoko	どこ doko
direction	こっち（こちら） kocchi（kochira）	そっち（そちら） socchi（sochira）	あっち（あちら） acchi（achira）	どっち（どちら） docchi（dochira）

Noun ＋ のV-方　　Noun ＋ no V-kata

このパソコンの使い方、わかりますか。　　Do you know how to use this computer?
Kono pasokon no tsukai-kata, wakarimasu ka.

この漢字の読み方を教えてください。　　Please tell me the reading for this kanji.
Kono kanji no yomi-kata o oshiete kudasai.

パソコンを使います　→　パソコンの使い方
Pasokon o tsukaimasu　　　Pasokon no tsukai-kata

漢字を読みます　→　漢字の読み方
Kanji o yomimasu　　　Kanji no yomi-kata

知っています　　shitte'imasu

A：えみさんのアドレス、知っていますか。　　Do you know Emi's address?
　　Emi-san no adoresu, shitte'imasu ka.

B：はい、知っています。これですよ。　　Yes, I do. Here it is.
　　Hai, shitte'imasu. Kore desu yo.

A：この漢字の読み方、知っていますか。　　Do you know the reading for this kanji?
　　Kono kanji no yomi-kata, shittei'masu ka.

B：すみません、わかりません。　　Sorry, I don't know.
　　Sumimasen, wakarimasen.

☺　A：パーティーの時間、知ってる？　　Do you know the time for the party?
　　　Pāthī no jikan, shitteru?

　　B：ごめん、知らない。　　Sorry, I don't know.
　　　Gomen, shiranai.

Noun ＋ の　　Noun ＋ no

A：それはえみさんの本ですか。　　Is that Emi's book?
　　Sore wa Emi-san no hon desu ka.

B：いいえ、えみさんのじゃないです。クリスさんのですよ。
　　Iie, Emi-san no janai desu. Kurisu-san no desu yo.
　　No, it's not Emi's. It's Chris'.

44

好きな ＋ noun　sukina ＋ noun

好きな映画を教えてください。
Sukina eiga o oshiete kudasai.

Please tell me your favorite movie.

好きな歌手はだれですか。
Sukina kashu wa dare desu ka.

Who is your favorite singer?

Particles

これは英語で何ですか。
Kore wa Eigo de nan desu ka.

What is this in English?

ここに本の名前を入れてください。
Koko ni hon no namae o irete kudasai.

Enter the name of a book here.

Notes　"よ yo" and "ね ne"　▶CD track 16

You probably hear a lot of people in Japanese conversations use "よ *yo*" or "ね *ne*" at the end of a sentence. "よ *yo*" and "ね *ne*" have the following meanings.

Use "よ *yo*" when you want to tell something to your speaking partner.

これ、おいしいですよ。
Kore, oishii desu yo.

This is delicious.

ここがAAレストランですよ。
Koko ga AA resutoran desu yo.

This is AA Restaurant.

Use "ね *ne*" when you want to share the same emotion as your speaking partner.

A：これ、おいしいですね。
Kore, oishii desu ne.

This is delicious, isn't it?

B：そうですね。おいしいですね。
Sō desu ne. Oishii desu ne.

Yeah, it is. It's yummy.

Use "よね *yone*" when you want to confirm something with your speaking partner or elicit a concurring opinion.

A：あの人、山田さんですよね。
Ano hito, Yamada-san desu yone.

That person is Yamada-san, right?

B：はい、そうです。
Hai, sō desu.

Yeah, that's right.

Exercise 1

Listen to conversations 1 through 6 and select the picture that matches each.

Ex. (c)
1. (   )   2. (   )   3. (   )   4. (   )   5. (   )

Exercise 2

First, study the verbs for Unit 3 and their conjugated froms in the vocabulary list. Then, look at the picture and form a sentence using "～てください ～*te kudasai*" as in the example.

Ex. 起きてください。
Okite kudasai.

1. この絵を
Kono e o

2. 電気を<ruby>電気<rt>でんき</rt></ruby>を
   Denki o _____

3. <ruby>毎日<rt>まいにち</rt></ruby>
   Mainichi _____

4. どうぞ、コーヒーを
   Dōzo, kōhī o _____

5. ちょっと
   Chotto _____

6. どうぞ、
   Dōzo, _____

7. ここに<ruby>名前<rt>なまえ</rt></ruby>を
   Koko ni namae o _____

Short Interview

As in the example, ask three people. Then expand the conversation to talk about whatever you want.

1. 週末の予定を教えてください。 　　　　Please tell me your plans for the weekend.
   Shūmatsu no yotei o oshiete kudasai.

2. ＿＿＿＿＿を教えてください。 　　　　Please tell me ＿＿＿＿.
   　　　　　o oshiete kudasai.

   Ex. 好きな映画を教えてください。 　　　Please tell me your favorite movie.
   　　Sukina eiga o oshiete kudasai.

名前	1の答え	2の答え

Preparation & Rehearsal

Leave the classroom in groups and take photos of Japanese writing you see around you on and off campus. If there are any Japanese people around as you do this, ask them about the reading or what it means.

Try to imagine the reading and meaning of the Japanese you photograph. In groups, practice asking and answering questions with each other. Use the following kinds of expressions.

この漢字の読み方は何ですか。　What is the reading for this kanji?
　Kono kanji no yomi-kata wa nan desu ka.

意味は何ですか。 　　　　　　　What is the meaning?
　Imi wa nan desu ka.

英語で何ですか。 　　　　　　　What is this in English?
　Eigo de nan desu ka.

例文を教えてください。 　　　　Please give me an example
　Reibun o oshiete kudasai. 　　　sentence.

ここに書いてください。 　　　　Please write it here.
　Koko ni kaite kudasai.

Real Session

Are you ready?

<ruby>日本<rt>に ほん</rt></ruby><ruby>語<rt>ご</rt></ruby><ruby>辞書<rt>じ しょ</rt></ruby>を<ruby>作<rt>つく</rt></ruby>ろう！　Make a Japanese dictionary!

Work together as a group to ask visitors questions and create Japanese dictionary complete with photos.

1. Paste each photo you took on a separate page, and create boxes for entering the readings, meanings, and example sentences.

2. Show the photos to a Japanese visitor, ask him or her the reading, English meanings and example sentences, and write them down.

3. Make a dictionary cover with the Japanese visitor.

--- **check** ---

1. Request something from a person.
   かんぺき　No problem □　　だいじょうぶ　OK □　　まだ　Not yet □
2. Recommend something to a person.
   かんぺき　No problem □　　だいじょうぶ　OK □　　まだ　Not yet □
3. Ask about things you do not understand and vocabulary.
   かんぺき　No problem □　　だいじょうぶ　OK □　　まだ　Not yet □

Empathetic listening is often heard in Japanese conversations. For example, listen to the following conversation.

Ex.

私、きのう新宿に行ったんですが（はい）、レストランに入ったら（ええ）、ジョニー・デップがいて（へええ）びっくりしました。

Watashi, kinō Shinjuku ni itta n desu ga（hai）, resutoran ni haittara（ee）, Joni Deppu ga ite（hee）bikkuri shimashita.

I went to Shinjuku yesterday (Yeah?), and when I entered a restaurant (Uh huh), I was surprised to find Johnny Depp was in there (Whoa!).

Empathetic listening is not answering questions. It shows that what your speaking partner is saying is getting through to you. It serves the same function as nodding your head.

In Japanese, there is different vocabulary for referring to one's own family members and another person's family members. However, this differentiation may not be present in casual conversation with friends and the like.

When talking about...	your family	someone's family
grandfather	そふ　sofu	おじいさん　ojīsan
grandmother	そぼ　sobo	おばあさん　obāsan
father	父 (ちち)　chichi	お父さん (とう)　otōsan
mother	母 (はは)　haha	お母さん (かあ)　okāsan
older brother	兄 (あに)　ani	お兄さん (にい)　onīsan
older sister	姉 (あね)　ane	お姉さん (ねえ)　onēsan
younger brother	弟 (おとうと)　otōto	弟さん (おとうと)　otōtosan
younger sister	妹 (いもうと)　imōto	妹さん (いもうと)　imōtosan
parents	りょうしん　ryōshin	ごりょうしん　go-ryōshin
brothers and sisters	きょうだい　kyōdai	ごきょうだい　go-kyōdai

Dialogue 1　▶CD track 19

〈Chris is showing a picture of his family to his teacher〉

Chris　：これがそふとそぼです。父 (ちち)のりょうしんです。

Kore ga sofu to sobo desu. Chichi no ryōshin desu.

This is my grandfather and grandmother. They're my father's parents.

Teacher：おじいさんとおばあさんはおいくつですか。

Ojīsan to obāsan wa o-ikutsu desu ka.

How old are your grandfather and grandmother?

Chris　：そふは72さい、そぼは70さいです。母 (はは)のりょうしんはイギリスにいます。これが父 (ちち)と母 (はは)です。

Sofu wa nanajūni-sai, sobo wa nanajussai desu. Haha no ryōshin wa Igirisu ni imasu. Kore ga chichi to haha desu.

My grandfather is 72 and my grandmother is 70. My mother's parents are in England. This is my father and mother.

Teacher：お父さん (とう)は背 (せ)が高 (たか)いですね。お母さん (かあ)はきれいですね。ごりょうしんはどちらに住 (す)んでいますか。

Otōsan wa se ga takai desu ne. Okāsan wa kirei desu ne. Goryoshin wa dochira ni sunde'imasu ka.

Your father is tall. Your mother is pretty. Where do your parents live?

Chris ：りょうしんは今フランスに住んでいます。

Ryōshin wa ima Furansu ni sunde'imasu.　My parents live in France now.

Teacher：この男の人は？

Kono otoko-no-hito wa?　Who is this man?

Chris ：それは兄です。中学校の先生です。

Sore wa ani desu. Chūgakkō no sensei desu.

That's my older brother. He's a junior high school teacher.

Teacher：この女の子は妹さん？ かわいいですね。

Kono onna-no-ko wa imōtosan? Kawaii desu ne.　Is this girl your little sister? She's cute.

Chris ：ええ、妹は10さい、小学生です。

Ee, imōto wa ju-ssai, shōgakusei desu.

Yes, my little sister is 10. She's an elementary school student.

▶ **See Vocabulary List, school**

Dialogue 2　▶ **CD track 20**　☺

〈Chris is showing a picture of his family to Emi〉

Chris：これ、ぼくの家族の写真。これがぼくのおじいちゃんとおばあちゃん*。

Kore, boku no kazoku no shashin. Kore ga boku no ojīchan to obāchan.

This is a photo of my family. This is my grandfather and grandmother.*

Emi ：おじいちゃんは<u>何</u>さい？

Ojīchan wa <u>nan-sai</u>?　How old is your grandfather?

*Using "ちゃん" adds a more casual nuance.

Chris：72さい。

Nanajūni-sai.　72.

Emi ：ふーん、おばあちゃんは？

Fūn, obāchan wa?　Hmm. How about your grandmother?

Chris：70さい。

Nanajussai.　70.

Emi ：おばあちゃん、わかいね。この人は、お父さんとお母さん？

Obāchan, wakai ne. Kono hito wa, otōsan to okāsan?

Your grandmother looks young. Is this your father and mother?

Chris：そう、2人は今フランスにいる。

Sō, futari wa ima Furansu ni iru.　Yes, they're both in France now.

Emi ：この人は？ お兄さん？ クリスにそっくり。

Kono hito wa? Onīsan? Kurisu ni sokkuri.

Who's this? Your older brother? He looks just like you, Chris.

Chris：そう？ ぼくのほうがかっこいいよ。

Sō? Boku <u>no hō ga</u> kakkoii yo.　Really? I'm better looking than him.

Unit **4**

Talking About Travel

―大阪はとても楽しかったです―

| Goals

1. Talk about where you went and what you did.

2. Introduce places and things.

3. Ask questions about other people's experiences and ask them their impressions.

Chris went on a trip to Osaka. He is talking with the teacher and his classmates about his trip to Osaka.

先週、ホストファミリーと<ruby>大阪<rt>おおさか</rt></ruby>に<ruby>行<rt>い</rt></ruby>きました。
これ、おみやげです。どうぞ。

Senshū, hosutofamirī to Ōsaka ni ikimashita.
Kore, omiyage desu. Dōzo.

I went to Osaka with my host family last week. This is a souvenir.
Here you go.

あ、どうもありがとう。<ruby>大阪<rt>おおさか</rt></ruby>はどうでしたか。

A, dōmo arigatō. Ōsaka wa dō deshita ka.

Oh, thank you. What was Osaka like?

とても<ruby>楽<rt>たの</rt></ruby>しかったです。<ruby>食<rt>た</rt></ruby>べ<ruby>物<rt>もの</rt></ruby>がおいしかったです。
たくさん<ruby>食<rt>た</rt></ruby>べました。

Totemo tanoshikatta desu. Tabemono ga oishikatta desu.
Takusan tabemashita.

It was really fun. The food was good.
I ate a bunch.

そうですか。<ruby>大阪<rt>おおさか</rt></ruby>でどこに<ruby>行<rt>い</rt></ruby>きましたか。

Sō desu ka. Ōsaka de doko ni ikimashita ka.

I see. Where did you go in Osaka?

まず、<ruby>大阪城<rt>おおさかじょう</rt></ruby>に<ruby>行<rt>い</rt></ruby>きました。それから、<ruby>町<rt>まち</rt></ruby>で<ruby>買<rt>か</rt></ruby>い<ruby>物<rt>もの</rt></ruby>をして、
ごはんを<ruby>食<rt>た</rt></ruby>べました。

Mazu, Ōsakajō ni ikimashita. Sorekara, machi de kaimono o shite,
gohan o tabemashita.

First, we went to Osaka Castle. After that, we did some shopping
in town and ate food.

東京から大阪までいくら？

Tōkyō kara Ōsaka made ikura?

How much does it cost from Tokyo to Osaka?

しんかんせんで30,000円ぐらい。ちょっと高いね。
東京から大阪まで、バスもあるよ。

Shinkansen de sanman-en gurai. Chotto takai ne. Tōkyō kara Ōsaka made, basu mo aru yo.

The Shinkansen was around 30,000 yen round-trip. It's kind of expensive. There are also buses from Tokyo to Osaka.

バスも高い？　　Is the bus expensive, too?

Basu mo takai?

バスは安いよ。8,000円ぐらい。でもおそい。9時間
ぐらいかかる。

Basu wa yasui yo. Hassen-en gurai. Demo osoi. Ku-jikan gurai kakaru.

The bus is cheap. Around 8,000 yen round-trip. But it's slow. It takes around nine hours.

クリスさんは大阪が好きですか。

Kurisu-san wa Ōsaka ga suki desu ka.

Chris, do you like Osaka?

はい、大好きです。また行きたいです。

Hai, daisuki desu. Mata ikitai desu.

Yes, I love it. I want to go there again.

い (i) -adjective sentence

[Nonpast]

大阪の食べ物はおいしいです。
Ōsaka no tabemono wa
oishii desu.

The food in Osaka is good.

大阪の食べ物はおいしくないです。
Ōsaka no tabemono wa
oishikunai desu.

The food in Osaka is not good.

[Past]

大阪の食べ物はおいしかったです。
Ōsaka no tabemono wa
oishikatta desu.

The food in Osaka was good.

大阪の食べ物はおいしくなかったです。
Ōsaka no tabemono wa
oishikunakatta desu.

The food in Osaka was not good.

おいしいラーメンを食べました。　I ate some yummy ramen.
Oishii rāmen o tabemashita.

な (na) adjective sentence

[Nonpast]

えみさんは元気です。
Emi-san wa genki desu.
Emi is feeling well.

えみさんは元気じゃないです。
Emi-san wa genki janai desu.
Emi is not feeling well.

[Past]

えみさんは元気でした。
Emi-san wa genki deshita.
Emi was feeling well.

えみさんは元気じゃなかったです。
Emi-san wa genki janakatta desu.
Emi was not feeling well.

元気な人が好きです。　I like happy people.
Genki na hito ga suki desu.

どうですか／どうでしたか　dō desu ka／dō deshita ka

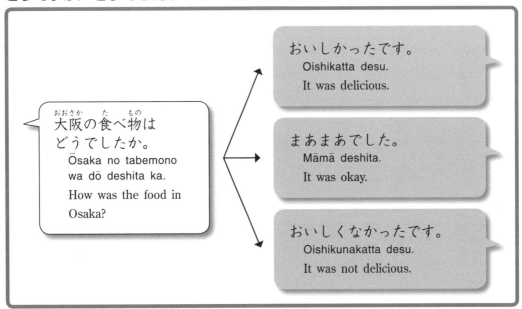

おおさか
大阪の食べ物は
どうでしたか。
Ōsaka no tabemono
wa dō deshita ka.
How was the food in
Osaka?

おいしかったです。
Oishikatta desu.
It was delicious.

まあまあでした。
Māmā deshita.
It was okay.

おいしくなかったです。
Oishikunakatta desu.
It was not delicious.

と（いっしょに）　to（issho ni）

おおさか　い
ホストファミリーと（いっしょに）大阪に行きました。
Hosutofamirī to（issho ni）Ōsaka ni ikimashita.
I went to Osaka（together）with my host family.

Conjunctions

おおさかじょう　い　　　　　　　　か　もの
まず、大阪城に行きました。それから、買い物をしました。
Mazu, ōsakajō ni ikimashita. Sorekara, kaimono o shimashita.
First, we went to Osaka Castle. After that, we did some shopping.

やす　　　　　　　　　　　　　　　　　　　　　おおさか
バスは安いです。でも、おそいです。だから、しんかんせんで大阪に
い
行きました。
Basu wa yasui desu. Demo, osoi desu. Dakara, shinkansen de Ōsaka ni ikimashita.
The bus is cheap. But it's slow. That's why we took the Shinkansen to Osaka.

Put actions in order

▶See p.105 for the te-form

大阪城を見て、買い物をして、ご飯を食べました。

Ōsakajō o mite, kaimono o shite, gohan o tabemashita.

We saw Osaka Castle, went shopping and ate food.

～から～まで　～kara～made

東京から大阪までいくらですか。

Tōkyō kara Osaka made ikura
desu ka.

How much does it cost from Tokyo
to Osaka?

スーパーは午後8時までです。

Sūpā wa gogo hachi-ji made desu.

The supermarket is open until 8 p.m.

～で　～de

しんかんせんで東京から大阪
まで30,000円ぐらいです。

Shinkansen de Tōkyō kara Ōsaka
made sanman-en gurai desu.

The Shinkansen from Tokyo to
Osaka is around 30,000 yen round-
trip.

＊歩いてホテルに行きました。

Aruite hoteru ni ikimashita.

We went to the hotel on foot.

どのぐらい　donogurai

A：大阪までどのぐらいですか。

Ōsaka made donogurai desu ka.

How long does it take to get to Osaka?

B：しんかんせんで3時間ぐらいです。

Shinkansen de san-jikan gurai desu.

About three hours on the Shinkansen.

V-たいです　V-tai desu

▶See p.104 for the masu-form

大阪に行きたいです。　　I want to go to Osaka.
Ōsaka ni ikitai desu.

すしを食べたいです。　　I want to eat sushi.
Sushi o tabetai desu.

Advanced

何か／何も　nani ka／nani mo

何か買いましたか。
Nani ka kaimashita ka.
Did you buy something?

はい、Tシャツを買いました。
Hai, T-shatsu o kaimashita.
Yes, I bought a T-shirt.

いいえ、何も買いませんでした。
Iie, nani mo kaimasen deshita.
No, I didn't buy anything.

Describe with multiple adjectives

[い (i) adjective]　大阪の食べ物は安くておいしいです。
Ōsaka no tabemono wa yasukute oishii desu.
Food is cheap and tasty in Osaka.

[な (na) adjective]　クリスさんは親切でかっこいいです。
Kurisu-san wa shinsetsu de kakkoii desu.
Chris is kind and good-looking.

～より／一番　～yori／ichiban

しんかんせんはバスより高いです。
Shinkansen wa basu yori takai desu.
The Shinkansen is more expensive than the bus.

ひこうきは一番高いです。
Hikōki wa ichiban takai desu.
A flight is the most expensive.

¥10,000.—　¥30,000.—　¥50,000.—

Noun＋ができます／Verb＋ことができます
Noun＋ga dekimasu／Verb＋koto ga dekimasu

私はサーフィンができます。　　I can surf.
Watashi wa sāfin ga dekimasu.

バスで大阪に行くことができます。　　You can take a bus to Osaka.
Basu de Ōsaka ni iku koto ga dekimasu.

▶See p.104 for the dictionary form

Informal adjective sentences ▶ CD track 22

い（i）adjective

[Nonpast]　おいしい　⇔　おいしくない
　　　　　　　oishii　　　　　　oishikunai

[Past]　　　おいしかった　⇔　おいしくなかった
　　　　　　　oishikatta　　　　　　oishikunakatta

な（na）adjective

[Nonpast]　元気（だ）　⇔　元気じゃない
　　　　　　　genki（da）　　　　　genki janai

[Past]　　　元気だった　⇔　元気じゃなかった
　　　　　　　genki datta　　　　　genki janakatta

これ、おいしい。
Kore, oishii.
This tastes good.

うん、おいしいね。
Un, oishii ne.
Mmm, yummy.

クリス、元気？
Kurisu, genki?
Chris, how are you?

うん、元気。
Un, genki.
Yeah, I'm fine.

大阪に行ったの？ どうだった？
Ōsaka ni itta no? Dō datta?
You went to Osaka? How was it?

うん、楽しかったよ。
Un, tanoshikatta yo.
Oh, it was fun.

Exercise 1

▶ CD track 23

First, study the adjectives in the vocabulary list for Unit 4. Then, listen to the recording and select the appropriate picture.

Ex. (d) 1. (   ) 2. (   ) 3. (   ) 4. (   ) 5. (   )
6. (   ) 7. (   )

a.

b.

c.

d.

e.

f.

g.

h.

Exercise 2

Answer to each question. Then, ask your classmates the same question.

1. 日本の生活はどうですか。　　How are you enjoying life in Japan?
   Nihon no seikatsu wa dō desu ka.

_____

2. どんな人が好きですか。　　What kind of people do you like?
   Donna hito ga suki desu ka.

_____

Make questions like those in Exercise 2 using "～はどうですか ～*wa dō desu ka*" and "どんな～が好きですか *donna ～ga suki desu ka*" and ask them to three people.

1. _____ はどうですか。

                                                     wa dō desu ka.

2. どんな_____ が好きですか。

   Donna   ga suki desu ka.

名前	1の答え	2の答え

Expand the conversation, as in the example.

Ex.

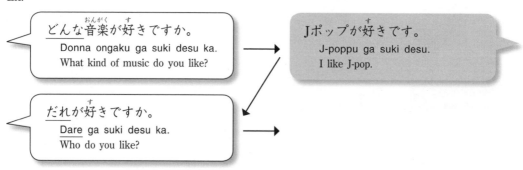

どんな音楽が好きですか。
Donna ongaku ga suki desu ka.
What kind of music do you like?

Jポップが好きです。
J-poppu ga suki desu.
I like J-pop.

だれが好きですか。
Dare ga suki desu ka.
Who do you like?

1. Prepare presentation photos.
2. Write a presentation script about a trip as you look at the below example from Chris' presentation.

大阪

こんにちは。クリスです。私は先週の週末、ホストファミリーと大阪に行きました。

Konnichiwa, Kurisu desu. Watashi wa senshū no shūmatsu, hosutofamirī to Ōsaka ni ikimashita.

しんかんせんで行きました。東京から大阪まで3時間ぐらいです。

Shinkansen de ikimashita. Tōkyō kara Ōsaka made san-jikan gurai desu.

大阪で、まず大阪城に行きました。写真を見てください。これは大阪城です。

Ōsaka de, mazu Ōsakajō ni ikimashita. Shashin o mite kudasai. Kore wa Ōsakajō desu.

大阪城は大きかったです。

Ōsakajō wa ōkikatta desu.

それから、私たちは買い物をして、昼ご飯を食べました。たこやきを食べました。おいしかったです。

Sorekara, watashitachi wa kaimono o shite, hirugohan o tabemashita. Takoyaki o tabemashita. Oishikatta desu.

…大阪の旅行はとても楽しかったです。また大阪に行きたいです。

Ōsaka no ryokō wa totemo tanoshikatta desu. Mata Ōsaka ni ikitai desu.

以上です。ありがとうございました。質問をお願いします。

Ijō desu. Arigatō gozaimashita. Shitsumon o onegaishimasu.

Hello. I'm Chris. Last weekend I went to Osaka with my host family. We went on the Shinkansen. It takes about three hours from Tokyo to Osaka. In Osaka, we first went to Osaka Castle. Look at this photo. This is Osaka Castle. Osaka Castle was big. Then we went shopping and ate lunch. We ate takoyaki. It was delicious. Our trip to Osaka was very fun. I want to go to Osaka again. That concludes my presentation. Thank you very much. Are there any questions?

---

3. Add captions in Japanese to your photos.
4. Use your script and photos to practice presenting with your classmates.
5. While looking at the Short Dialogues, practice post-presentation Q&A with your classmates.

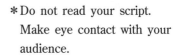 (Are you ready?)

Real Session

 発表しよう！ Give a presentation!

Give a presentation about a place you have been to in Japan. It can be anything: a long trip, a daytrip, an event, shopping, whatever.

> Form small groups, including visitors. (Or you can present in front of the entire class.)

> Each person will give a presentation while showing his or her photos (slides).

*Do not read your script. Make eye contact with your audience.

> You will field questions and comments from visitors and classmates. Answer their questions.

*Make an active effort to ask questions when your classmate present.

> When everyone has finished presenting, engage in open conversation with the visitors. Try asking them about things like sightseeing spots in Japan and their travel experiences.

Make good preparations for your presentation and practice it a lot. You will feel more confident if you and your classmates work together to predict what questions will come up. If you prepare well, you will not be nervous!

Don't panic even if you cannot understand a question from the audience! You'll be fine so long as you relax.

When you understand a question just a little, indicate that you partially get it. Otherwise the asker might think you did not understand at all and give up on communicating with you.

1. Repeat the part you understood（with rising intonation）.

    Question：大阪の食べ物は×××？　←The ×'s are the part you didn't catch.

        You：大阪の食べ物は…？

            Osaka no tabemono wa ...?

2. Ask about words you do not know.

    ×××は何ですか。　What is ×××?

    ××× wa nan desu ka.

3. If you understand the question but do not know how to answer, indicate that. Do not just say "わかりません *wakarimasen*".

    Question：大阪の食べ物は おいしかったですか。

            Osaka no tabemono wa oishikatta desu ka.

            Was the food in Osaka good?

        You：わかりません。大阪で何も食べませんでした。

            Wakarimasen. Osaka de nani mo tabemasen deshita.

            I don't know. I didn't eat anything in Osaka.

▶ **See p.23 KAIWA master!**

No matter what you do, do not be silent. Show what you understand and try to keep the conversation going! You can do it!

--- check --

1. Talk about where you went and what you did.

    かんぺき　No problem ☐　　だいじょうぶ　OK ☐　　まだ　Not yet ☐

2. Introduce places and things.

    かんぺき　No problem ☐　　だいじょうぶ　OK ☐　　まだ　Not yet ☐

3. Ask questions about other people's experiences and ask them their impressions.

    かんぺき　No problem ☐　　だいじょうぶ　OK ☐　　まだ　Not yet ☐

Expressions

頭
あたま
atama   head

のど
nodo   throat

おなか
onaka   stomach

は
ha   tooth

がいたいです
ga itai desu
hurts

くしゃみ
kushami   sneeze

げり
geri   loose bowels

やけど
yakedo   burned/a burn

けが
kega   hurt/an injury

をします
o shimasu
get/have

気持ちが悪いです   feel sick
きもち   わる
kimochi ga warui desu

せきが出ます   have a cough
で
seki ga demasu

かぜをひきます   catch a cold
kaze o hikimasu

薬を飲みます   take medicine
くすり の
kusuri o nomimasu

ねつがあります   have a fever
netsu ga arimasu

▶ See Vocabulary List, body

Dialogue   ▶ CD track 25

〈At a hospital〉

Doctor ：どうしましたか。
Dō shimashita ka.   What happened?

Chris ：頭がいたいです。ねつもあります。
あたま
Atama ga itai desu. Netsu mo arimasu.
My head hurts. I have a fever, too.

Doctor ：せきはどうですか。
Seki wa dō desu ka.   Do you have a cough?

Chris ：せきも出ます。のどがいたいです。
で
Seki mo demasu. Nodo ga itai desu.   Yes, I do. My throat hurts.

Doctor ：かぜですね。この薬を１日３回飲んでください。
くすり にち かい の
今日は早くねてください。お大事に。
きょう はや   だいじ
Kaze desu ne. Kono kusuri o ichi-nichi san-kai nonde kudasai. Kyo wa hayaku nete kudasai. Odaijini.
You have a cold. Take this medicine three times a day. Go to bed early today. Take care.

Chris ：はい、ありがとうございました。
Hai, arigatō gozaimashita.   Okay, thank you.

Heading Around Town
―あのシャツを見たいんですが―

Goals

1. Ask a stranger for directions, a request and permission.
2. Politely decline a request.
3. Do shopping that requires conversation.

Short Dialogues

〈While shopping〉

あのー、すみません。ABCモールは
どうやって行きますか。
Anō, sumimasen. ABC mōru wa dōyatte ikimasu ka.
Um, excuse me. How do I get to ABC Mall?

あのバスですよ。　　On that bus.
Ano basu desu yo.

わかりました。どうもありがとうございました。
Wakarimashita. Dōmo arigatō gozaimashita.
I see. Thank you very much.

すみません。このバスはABCモールに行きま
すか。
Sumimasen. Kono basu wa ABC mōru ni ikimasu ka.
Excuse me. Does this bus go to ABC Mall?

はい、行きますよ。　　Yes, it does.
Hai, ikimasu yo.

· ·

〈At a clothing store〉

あのー、すみません。あのシャツを見たい
んですが…。
Ano, sumimasen. Ano shatsu o
mitai n desu ga...
Um, excuse me. I would like to look at that
shirt…

はい、どうぞ。　Sure, go ahead.
Hai, dōzo.

しちゃく、いいですか。　May I try it on?
Shichaku, ii desu ka.

はい。どうぞ、こちらです。
Hai. Dōzo, kochira desu.
Sure, go ahead. Over here.

いかがですか。　Do you like it?
Ikaga desu ka.

はい、ちょうどいいです。これ、ください。
Hai, chōdo ii desu. Kore, kudasai.
Yes, it's just right. I'll take this.

・・・・・・・・・・・・・・・・・・・・・・・・・・・・・・

あのー、すみません。食べ物はちょっと…。
Anō, sumimasen. Tabemono wa chotto...
Um, excuse me, but your food…

あ、はい。すみません。
A, hai. Sumimasen.
Oh, yes. We're sorry.

• Expressions

どうやって ＋ verb   dōyatte ＋ verb

A：ABCモールはどうやって行きますか。

ABC mōru wa dōyatte ikimasu ka.

How do I get to ABC Mall?

B：あの3番のバスですよ。10分ぐらいです。

Ano san-ban no basu desu yo. Juppun gurai desu.

Take that Number 3 bus. It takes about ten minutes.

A：これはどうやって使いますか。

Kore wa dōyatte tsukaimasu ka.

How do I use this?

B：水はこのボタンですよ。

Mizu wa kono botan desu yo.

This button is for water.

V-たいんですが…   V-tai n desu ga...

▶ See p.104 for the masu-form

A：すみません。あのシャツを見たいんですが…。

Sumimasen. Ano shatsu o mitai n desu ga...

Excuse me. I would like to look at that shirt...

B：はい。少々お待ちください。

Hai. Shōshō omachi kudasai.

Okay. Just a moment, please.

A：すみません。ちょっと聞きたいんですが…。
ゆうびんきょくはどこですか。

Sumimasen. Chotto kikitai n desu ga... Yūbinkyoku wa doko desu ka.

Excuse me. I'd like to ask something... Where is the post office?

B：ゆうびんきょくは、あの白い建物ですよ。

Yūbinkyoku wa, ano shiroi tatemono desu yo.

The post office is that white building over there.

▶ See p.79 KAIWA master! for incomplete sentences.

Asking for directions

A：ABCモール
ABC mōru

はどこですか。
wa doko desu ka.

Where is 〜?

はどうやって行きますか。
wa dōyatte ikimasu ka.

How do I get to 〜?

に行きたいんですが…。
ni ikitai n desu ga...

I want to go to 〜…

B：まっすぐ行って、銀行を右にまがってください。
Massugu itte, ginkō o migi ni magatte kudasai.
Go straight and turn right at the bank.

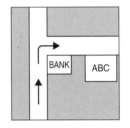

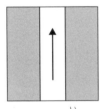

まっすぐ行く
massugu iku
Go straight

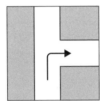

右にまがる
migi ni magaru
Turn right

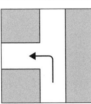

左にまがる
hidari ni magaru
Turn left

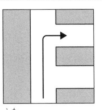

2つめのかどを
右にまがる
futatsume no kado o
migi ni magaru
Turn right at the second corner

Noun、いいですか　Noun, ii desu ka

You can also use "いいですか *ii desu ka*" to ask for permission or make a request.

A：しちゃく、いいですか。
Shichaku, ii desu ka.

May I try this on?

B：はい。どうぞ、こちらへ。
Hai. Dōzo, kochira e.

Sure, go ahead. Over here.

A：先生、すみません。トイレ、いいですか。
Sensei, sumimasen. Toire, ii desu ka.

Excuse me, sir/ma'am. May I go to the restroom?

B：はい、どうぞ。
Hai, dōzo.

Yes, you may.

A : すみません。写真、いいですか。
　　Sumimasen. Shashin, ii desu ka.

　　Excuse me. Can you take our picture?

B : はい、いいですよ。
　　Hai, ii desu yo.

　　Sure, no problem.

A : ありがとうございます。お願いします。
　　Arigatō gozaimasu. Onegaishimasu.

　　Thank you very much.

Noun ＋ はちょっと…　Noun ＋ wa chotto...

▶ See p.79 KAIWA master!

A : あのー、すみません。食べ物はちょっと…。
　　Anō, sumimasen. Tabemono wa chotto...

　　Um, excuse me, but your food…

B : あ、すみません。
　　A, sumimasen.

　　Oh, I'm sorry.

A : あのー、写真、いいですか。
　　Anō, shashin, ii desu ka.

　　Um, can we take a picture?

B : あ、すみません。写真はちょっと…。
　　A, sumimasen. Shashin wa chotto...

　　Um, sorry, but no pictures…

A : あした、映画に行きませんか。
　　Ashita, eiga ni ikimasen ka.

　　Do you want to go see a movie tomorrow?

B : あ、あしたはちょっと…。テストの勉強をします。
　　A, ashita wa chotto...Tesuto no benkyō o shimasu.

　　Ah, tomorrow isn't good for me…I'm going to study for a test.

A : あ、そうですか。じゃあ、また今度。　Oh, I see. Well, next time, then.
　　A, sō desu ka. Jā, mata kondo.

<ruby>同<rt>おな</rt></ruby>じです／ちがいます　onaji desu／chigaimasu

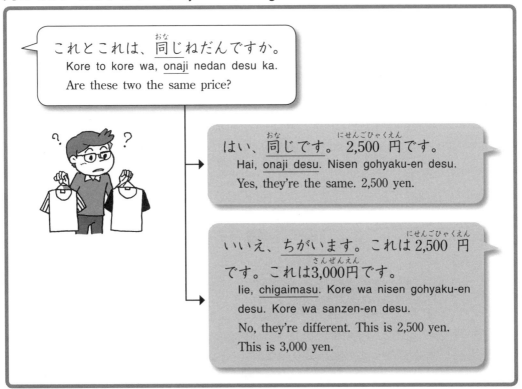

これとこれは、<ruby>同<rt>おな</rt></ruby>じねだんですか。
Kore to kore wa, onaji nedan desu ka.
Are these two the same price?

はい、<ruby>同<rt>おな</rt></ruby>じです。2,500<ruby>円<rt>にせんごひゃくえん</rt></ruby>です。
Hai, onaji desu. Nisen gohyaku-en desu.
Yes, they're the same. 2,500 yen.

いいえ、ちがいます。これは2,500<ruby>円<rt>にせんごひゃくえん</rt></ruby>です。これは3,000<ruby>円<rt>さんぜんえん</rt></ruby>です。
Iie, chigaimasu. Kore wa nisen gohyaku-en desu. Kore wa sanzen-en desu.
No, they're different. This is 2,500 yen. This is 3,000 yen.

Notes　Cash Register Conversations

You may be asked various questions when you buy something at a convenience store.

おはしは？
O-hashi wa?

スプーンは？
Supūn wa?

ふくろは？
Fukuro wa?

あたためますか？
Atatamemasu ka?

At a drug store or electronic store you may be asked, "ポイントカードを<ruby>作<rt>つく</rt></ruby>りますか *Pointokādo o tsukurimasu ka* (Would you like to make a point card?)". A point card collects points for you each time you make a purchase. You can buy something with your points once you collect enough.

・When you want one.　はい、お<ruby>願<rt>ねが</rt></ruby>いします。　Hai, onegaishimasu.
・When you do not need one.　いいえ、けっこうです／いりません。 Iie, kekkō desu / Irimasen.
＊ "いいです *ii desu*" can be taken both ways, so be careful.

Listen to the conversation and select the correct answer: A or B.

Ex. (a) **a.**  **b.**

1. ( ) **a.**  **b.**

2. ( ) **a.**  **b.**

3. ( ) **a.**  **b.**

4. ( ) **a.** 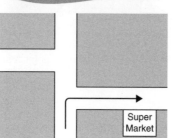 **b.**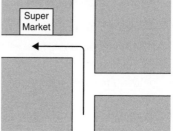

Exercise 2

What do you say? After you write it down, pair up with a classmate and practice the conversation.

1.

しお、
Shio, _____

2.

このCDを
Kono CD o _____

すみません。しゅくだいをわすれました。
Sumimasen. Shukudai o wasuremashita.

3. _____

ごめんね。
Gomenne.

4. _____

5. _____

6. _____

Short Interview

Ask three people about where they have gone out recently. Also ask how they went to those places. Then expand the conversation to discuss whatever you want.

Ex.　A：最近、どこに行きましたか。　Where have you been lately?

Saikin, doko ni ikimashita ka.

　　B：ディズニーランドに行きました。　I went to Disneyland.

Dhizunīrando ni ikimashita.

　　A：どうやって行きましたか。　How did you go?

Dōyatte ikimashita ka.

　　B：電車で行きました。京葉線の舞浜駅です。

Densha de ikimashita. Keiyō-sen no Maihama-eki desu.

I took the train. It's by Maihama Station on the Keiyo Line.

名前	場所の名前	どうやって行く？

Do a role play with a classmate trying on clothes at a clothing store. First, the customer will ask if he or she can try on some clothes. The clerk guide the customer to the changing room. After trying on the clothes, refer to the following examples and practice various patterns.

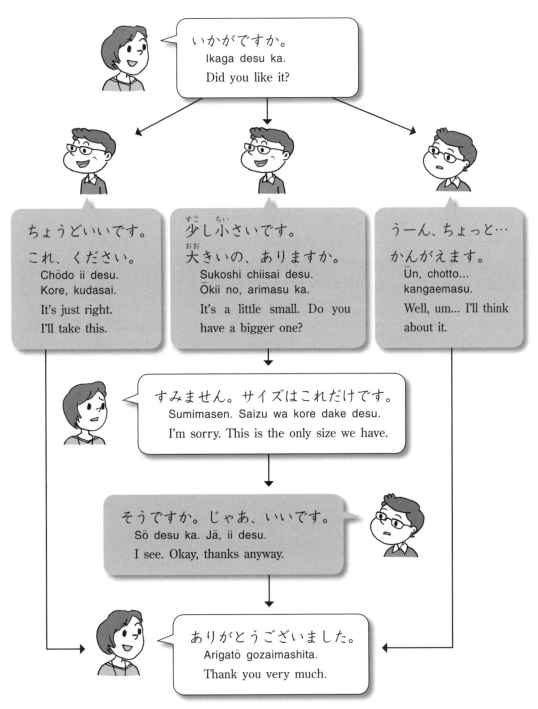

いかがですか。
Ikaga desu ka.
Did you like it?

ちょうどいいです。
これ、ください。
Chōdo ii desu.
Kore, kudasai.
It's just right.
I'll take this.

少し小さいです。
大きいの、ありますか。
Sukoshi chiisai desu.
Ōkii no, arimasu ka.
It's a little small. Do you have a bigger one?

うーん、ちょっと…
かんがえます。
Ūn, chotto...
kangaemasu.
Well, um... I'll think about it.

すみません。サイズはこれだけです。
Sumimasen. Saizu wa kore dake desu.
I'm sorry. This is the only size we have.

そうですか。じゃあ、いいです。
Sō desu ka. Jā, ii desu.
I see. Okay, thanks anyway.

ありがとうございました。
Arigatō gozaimashita.
Thank you very much.

Real Session

Are you ready?

服を買いに行こう！ Let's go buy some clothes!

In groups, go to a local clothing store and try on lots of things. Try talking a bunch with the clerks there!

> Form groups and decide store to go to.

> Go to the store as a group.

> Each of you will find clothes you want to try on and ask a clerk if you can try them.

> Just like you practiced, tell the clerk what size, color, design and whatnot that you want and try some things on.

> If you like something, buy it. Of course it's okay if you don't buy anything.

> Report back at the class. Which store did you go to? What kinds of clothes did you try on? What did you buy? If you did not buy anything, then why?

＊Choose a date and time when you do not expect the store to be crowded.

Unlike a supermarket or convenience store, you can practice speaking Japanese a lot at a clothing store. Take advantage of this opportunity, but without annoying the staff.

When you call out to a person, ask for permission, make a request, or find it hard to say "No", speak gently so as not to be rude.

1. Start speak with a phrase like "あのー *anō*" and "すみません *sumimasen*".

   あのー、すみません。写真、いいですか。

   　　Anō, sumimasen. Shashin, ii desu ka.

   　　Um, excuse me. Can I take a picture? / Can you take my picture?

2. Use "ちょっと *chotto*".

   Ａ：あした、ひまですか。　　　　　　Are you free tomorrow?
   　　Ashita, hima desu ka.

   Ｂ：すみません。あしたはちょっと…。　　Sorry, but not tomorrow...
   　　Sumimasen, ashita wa chotto...

3. Use incomplete sentences. Incomplete sentences sound more gentle than complete sentences.

   すみません。ちょっと、聞きたいんですが…。

   　　Sumimasen. Chotto, kikitai n desu ga...

   　　Excuse me. I' d like to ask something...

--- **check** ---

1. Ask a stranger for directions, a request and permission.
   　かんぺき No problem □　　だいじょうぶ OK □　　まだ Not yet □
2. Politely decline a request.
   　かんぺき No problem □　　だいじょうぶ OK □　　まだ Not yet □
3. Do shopping that requires conversation.
   　かんぺき No problem □　　だいじょうぶ OK □　　まだ Not yet □

Saying Goodbye

―日本語を教えてくれて、ありがとう―

Goals

1. Express your gratitude to a person for his/her kindness during your stay in Japan.

2. Talk about your memories of Japan.

3. Talk about your future plans or dreams.

〈At a farewell party〉

クリスさんはいつアメリカに帰りますか。
Kurisu-san wa itsu Amerika ni kaerimasu ka.
When will you go back to America, Chris?

来週の日曜日に帰ります。先生、いろいろありがとうござい
ました。クラスはとても楽しかったです。たくさん、日本語
を勉強しました。
Raishū no nichiyōbi ni kaerimasu. Sensei, iroiro arigatō gozaimashita.
Kurasu wa totemo tanoshikatta desu. Takusan, nihon-go o benkyō
shimashita.
I will go back next Sunday. Thank you so much for everything, sir/
ma'am. The class was really fun. I learned a lot of Japanese.

それはよかったです。これからもがんばってくださいね。
お元気で。
Sore wa yokatta desu. Korekara mo ganbatte kudasai ne.
O-genki de.
That's good. Keep studying hard. Take care.

はい、先生もお元気で。
Hai, sensei mo o-genki de.
Yeah, you too, sir/ma'am.

日本はどうでしたか。
Nihon wa dō deshita ka.
How did you like Japan?

とても楽しかったです。たくさん友だちを作りました。そして、いろいろなけいけんをしました。
Totemo tanoshikatta desu. Takusan tomodachi o tsukurimashita. Soshite, iroiro na keiken o shimashita.
It was very fun. I made a lot of friends. And I had many experiences.

クリスさん、また日本に来ますか。
Kurisu-san, mata Nihon ni kimasu ka.
Will you come to Japan again, Chris?

はい、また来たいです。来年の夏に大学をそつぎょうしたら、もう一度日本に来て、日本ではたらきたいです。
Hai, mata kitai desu. Rainen no natsu ni daigaku o sotsugyō shitara, mō ichido Nihon ni kite, Nihon de hatarakitai desu.
Yes, I want to come again. In the summer of next year, after I graduate from college, I want to come to Japan again and work in Japan.

· ·

クリスさん、もう、おみやげを買いましたか。
Kurisu-san, mō, omiyage o kaimashita ka.
Did you already buy souvenirs, Chris?

いいえ、まだです。あした買います。
Iie, mada desu. Ashita kaimasu.
No, not yet. I'll buy them tomorrow.

しょうた、しゅくだいをてつだってくれて、
ありがとう。アメリカに来たら、れんらくしてね。

Shōta, shukudai o tetsudatte kurete, arigatō. Amerika ni kitara, renraku shite ne.

Thank you for helping me with my homework, Shota. Get in touch if you come to America.

うん。れんらくするよ。クリスも元気で。

Un, renraku suru yo. Kurisu mo genki de.

Yes, I will. Take care, Chris.

シンさん、みんなといっしょに日本語を勉強して、
楽しかったね。

Shin-san, minna to issho ni Nihon-go o benkyō shite, tanoshikatta ne.

It was fun studying Japanese with everyone, wasn't it, Shin?

うん。旅行も楽しかったね。またメールするね。

Un, ryokō mo tanoshikatta ne. Mata mēru suru ne.

Yep. Traveling was fun, too. I'll email you later.

うん、またね。

Un, matane.

Okay. See ya.

V-たら、～　V-tara, ～

▶ See p.104 for the ta-form

大学をそつぎょうした<u>ら</u>、また日本に来たいです。

Daigaku o sotsugyō shi<u>tara</u>, mata Nihon ni kitai desu.

After I graduate from college, I want to come to Japan again.

（もし）アメリカに来た<u>ら</u>、れんらくしてね。

(Moshi) Amerika ni ki<u>tara</u>, renraku shite ne.

If you come to America, get in touch with me.

（もし）きかいがあった<u>ら</u>、テキサスに来てください。

(Moshi) kikai ga at<u>tara</u>, Tekisasu ni kite kudasai.

If you have the chance, please come to Texas.

もう／まだ　mō／mada

もうおみやげを買いましたか。

<u>Mō</u> omiyage o kaimashita ka.

Have you already bought souvenirs?

はい、<u>もう</u>買いました。

Hai, <u>mō</u> kaimashita.

Yes, I've already bought them.

いいえ、<u>まだ</u>です。

Iie, <u>mada</u> desu.

No, not yet.

私、<u>もう</u>昼ごはん食べたよ。

Watashi, <u>mō</u> hirugohan tabeta yo.

I've already eaten lunch.

私は<u>まだ</u>。

Watashi wa <u>mada</u>.

I haven't yet.

V-てくれて、ありがとう（ございます／ございました）
V-te kurete, arigatō（gozaimasu／gozaimashita）

▶ See p.105 for the te-form

しゅくだいをてつだって<u>くれて、ありがとう</u>。

Shukudai o tetsudatte <u>kurete, arigatō</u>.

Thanks for helping me with my homework.

毎<small>まいにち</small>日おいしいご飯<small>はん</small>を作<small>つく</small>って<u>くれて</u>、

ありがとうございました。

Mainichi oishii gohan o tsukutte <u>kurete</u>,

<u>arigatō gozaimashita</u>.

Thank you for making delicious meals every day.

Advanced

Verb ＋とき／Noun ＋のとき　Verb ＋ toki／Noun ＋ no toki

また日本<small>にほん</small>に来<small>く</small>る<u>とき</u>、れんらくします。

▶ See p.105 for the dictionary form

Mata Nihon ni kuru <u>toki</u>, renraku shimasu.

Get in touch when you come to Japan again.

子<small>こ</small>ども<u>のとき</u>、よく日本<small>にほん</small>のまんがを読<small>よ</small>みました。

Kodomo <u>no toki</u>, yoku Nihon no manga o yomimashita.

I read a lot of Japanese comics when I was a kid.

V-なければなりません　V-nakereba narimasen

Ａ：来年<small>らいねん</small>の夏休<small>なつやす</small>みに日本<small>にほん</small>に来<small>き</small>ますか。

Rainen no natsuyasumi ni Nihon ni kimasu ka.

Will you come to Japan during summer vacation next year?

Ｂ：来<small>き</small>たいです。でも、夏休<small>なつやす</small>みはアルバイトを<u>しなければなりません</u>。

Kitai desu. Demo, natsuyasumi wa arubaito o <u>shinakereba narimasen</u>.

I want to come. But I have to work a part-time job during summer vacation.

▶ See p.105 for the nai-form

V-たことがあります　V-ta koto ga arimasu

富士山_{ふ じ さん}に行_いったことがありますか。
Fujisan ni itta koto ga arimasu ka.
Have you been to Mt. Fuji?

はい、あります。
Hai, arimasu.
Yes, I have.

いいえ、ありません。
Iie, arimasen.
No, I haven't.

▶ See p.104 for the ta-form

～（だ）と思_{おも}います　～（da）to omoimasu

日本_{に ほん}はきれいな国_{くに}だと思_{おも}います。
Nihon wa kirei na kuni da to omoimasu.
I think Japan is a beautiful country.

日本語_{に ほん ご}はとてもおもしろいと思_{おも}います。
Nihon-go wa totemo omoshiroi to omoimasu.
I think the Japanese language is very interesting.

N o t e s "がんばって ganbatte"

You have probably noticed that Japanese people often say "がんばって *ganbatte*" or "がんばってください *ganbatte kudasai*". They especially say it a lot when saying goodbye. The literal meaning is "Work hard", but it does not necessarily mean this since the expression is actually used like "Good luck!" in English. You do not have to think, "Why do I have to work harder when I am already working this hard?" or "Do they think I am not working hard?". Take it in a positive way.

がんばって！

がんばって
ください！

Listen to the speakers and write down their memories of Japan and future plans.

	名前	Memories of Japan	Future Plans
1.	クリス Kurisu		
2.	シン Shin		
3.	カルロス Karurosu		
4.	アート Āto		

Exercise 2

Write down your memories of Japan. Try to remember lots of things, like Japanese classes, studying, friends, your host family, the dorm, travel, Japanese culture and society, etc. Use as much of the Japanese you have studied as you can.

Make two questions about future plans and ask them to three people.

Ex. 国に帰ったら、何をしますか。　　　　What will you do when you go back home?
　　Kuni ni kaettara, nani o shimasu ka.

　　しょうらい、何をしたいですか。　　　What do you want to do in the future?
　　Shōrai, nani o shitai desu ka.

1. _____

2. _____

名前	1の答え	2の答え

Try to expand the conversation!

Ex. A：しょうらい、何をしたいですか。
　　　　Shōrai, nani o shitai desu ka.
　　　　What do you want to do in the future?

　　B：ゲームを作りたいです。
　　　　Gēmu o tsukuritai desu.
　　　　I want to make video games.

　　A：どんなゲームを作りたいですか。
　　　　Donna gēmu o tsukuritai desu ka.
　　　　What kinds of video games do you want to make?

　　B：サムライのロールプレイングゲームを作りたいです。
　　　　Samurai no rōru-pureingu-gēmu o tsukuritai desu.
　　　　I want to make samurai role-playing games.

Preparation & Rehearsal

1. Refer to Chris' email and write a thank-you email or card to a person who has been kind to you, such as your host family, a teacher, a friend or a member of the school's administrative staff.

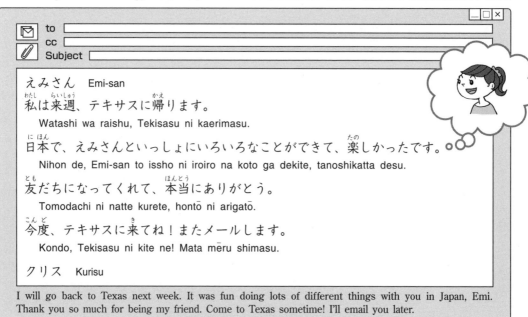

to
cc
Subject

えみさん　Emi-san

私は来週、テキサスに帰ります。
わたし　らいしゅう　　　　　　かえ

Watashi wa raishu, Tekisasu ni kaerimasu.

日本で、えみさんといっしょにいろいろなことができて、楽しかったです。
にほん　　　　　　　　　　　　　　　　　　　　　　　　たの

Nihon de, Emi-san to issho ni iroiro na koto ga dekite, tanoshikatta desu.

友だちになってくれて、本当にありがとう。
とも　　　　　　　　　ほんとう

Tomodachi ni natte kurete, hontō ni arigatō.

今度、テキサスに来てね！またメールします。
こんど　　　　　　き

Kondo, Tekisasu ni kite ne! Mata mēru shimasu.

クリス　Kurisu

I will go back to Texas next week. It was fun doing lots of different things with you in Japan, Emi. Thank you so much for being my friend. Come to Texas sometime! I'll email you later.

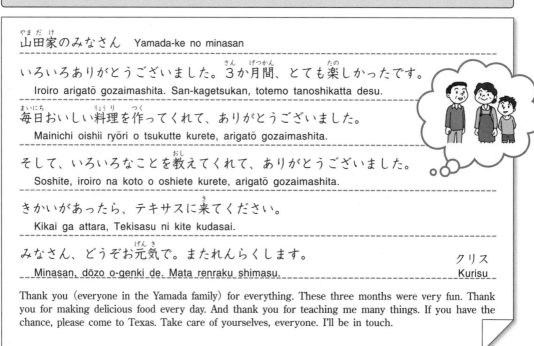

山田家のみなさん　Yamada-ke no minasan
やまだけ

いろいろありがとうございました。3か月間、とても楽しかったです。
　　　　　　　　　　　　　　　　　さん　げつかん　　　たの

Iroiro arigatō gozaimashita. San-kagetsukan, totemo tanoshikatta desu.

毎日おいしい料理を作ってくれて、ありがとうございました。
まいにち　　　りょうり　つく

Mainichi oishii ryōri o tsukutte kurete, arigatō gozaimashita.

そして、いろいろなことを教えてくれて、ありがとうございました。
　　　　　　　　　　おし

Soshite, iroiro na koto o oshiete kurete, arigatō gozaimashita.

きかいがあったら、テキサスに来てください。
　　　　　　　　　　　　　　　　き

Kikai ga attara, Tekisasu ni kite kudasai.

みなさん、どうぞお元気で。またれんらくします。
　　　　　　　　げんき

Minasan, dōzo o-genki de. Mata renraku shimasu.

クリス
Kurisu

Thank you (everyone in the Yamada family) for everything. These three months were very fun. Thank you for making delicious food every day. And thank you for teaching me many things. If you have the chance, please come to Texas. Take care of yourselves, everyone. I'll be in touch.

2. Together with a classmate, practice talking about what you are grateful for and your memories about your time in Japan as you look at the Short Dialogues on p.82-84.

Real Session

Are you ready?

日本(にほん)の思(おも)い出(で)を話(はな)そう！　Let's talk about our memories of Japan!

How has your time in Japan been? Talk with a visitor about your memories of Japan and plans for the future.

1. Form small groups, including visitors.

2. Engage in open conversation about your memories of Japan, such as Japanese classes, studying, travel, friends, your host family, the dorm or Japanese culture and society.

*Use as much of the Japanese you have studied as you can. You can show photos or other visual aids if you like.

3. Engage in open conversation about your dreams or plans for the future.

*Try to ask questions about your classmates' dreams and plans, too.

4. If a visitor is a person who has been kind to you in some way, express your gratitude and give that person your card.

Some good ways to keep the conversation going are...

1. Make good use of question words.

Try and ask your speaking partner questions by making good use of question words like "何 *nani*／何 *nan*", "だれ *dare*", "どこ *doko*", "いつ *itsu*", "どうやって *dōyatte*", "どんな *donna*" and "どうして *dōshite*".

それは何ですか。
Sore wa nan desu ka.

どうしてですか。
Dōshite desu ka.

どんな映画ですか。
Donna eiga desu ka.

どこですか。
Doko desu ka.

2. Show interest in what your speaking partner says.

If your speaking partner is interested in what you are saying, it will encourage you to speak, right? Try using expressions like "そうですか *sō desu ka* (Is that so?)", "そうですね *sō desu ne* (That's right.)", "本当ですか *hontō desu ka* (Really?)", "おもしろいですね *omoshiroi desu ne* (That's interesting.)", "すごいですね *sugoi desu ne* (That's amazing!)" and "いいですね *ii desu ne* (That's nice.)". With friends you can use expressions like "へえー *hē*", "そうなんだ *sōnanda*", "本当？ *hontō?*", and the following expressions.

本当？
Hontō?

すごい！
Sugoi!

おもしろいね。
Omoshiroi ne.

私も見たい！
Watashi mo mitai!

--- **check** --

1. Express your gratitude to a person for his/her kindness during your stay in Japan.

   かんぺき No problem ☐   だいじょうぶ OK ☐   まだ Not yet ☐

2. Talk about your memories of Japan.

   かんぺき No problem ☐   だいじょうぶ OK ☐   まだ Not yet ☐

3. Talk about your future plans or dreams.

   かんぺき No problem ☐   だいじょうぶ OK ☐   まだ Not yet ☐

Appendix

Distinctive Features of the Japanese Language

I. Pronunciation

Japanese has five vowels and is primarily pronounced in consonant + vowel sets. The vowel sound is often not pronounced (e.g. the underlined part of *kakimasu* is often silent), but this can depend on differences between regional dialects and individual people. It does not affect the meaning, so you do not have to worry about it much.

Special sounds are long vowels, double consonants and the kana ん ("*n*") (e.g. *Tōkyō, shusshin, Nihon-go*). Listen carefully to the pronunciation from your teachers and CDs and practice it.

Each word has a fixed high-low accent. This helps differentiate between homonyms.

あめ ame (rain) ⇔ あめ ame (candy)   さけ sake (salmon) ⇔ さけ sake (alcohol)

You can check words' accents with dictionaries and websites. Accents are also different between dialects, but the voices recorded for this textbook are spoken with the common accent used in and around Tokyo.

II. Writing System

1. Types of Characters

Japanese has three types of characters: hiragana, katakana and kanji. Hiragana and katakana are phonetic, i.e. they represent sounds. As you can see on the inside covers, hiragana and katakana are organized in the same system. Generally, there is one hiragana and one katakana for each sound. Kanji are logograms that represent both sounds and meanings.

2. The Roles of the Three Character Types

Katakana is primarily used to write loanwords and foreign names. Kanji are normally used in parts of words that express the real meaning, such as names, nouns and verb/adjective stems. Hiragana is used for other functional word parts (conjugations, particles, etc.).

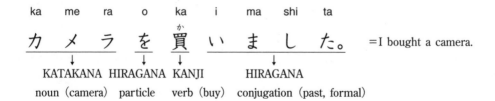

In the sentence above, "カメラ kamera" is in katakana since it is a loanword, the verb stem representing "buy" is a kanji and the particle and verb conjugation are written as hiragana.

3. Kanji Readings

A single kanji typically has two readings, the *kunyomi* and the *onyomi*, and may have even more sounds. For example, the meaning of the kanji "山" is "mountain", while the readings include "やま *yama*" (kun'yomi) and "さん *san*" (on'yomi). Generally, the kun'yomi is an originally Japanese sound given to a kanji, while the on'yomi is the reading that came over from China along with the kanji long ago. The reading is determined by the situation or word the kanji is used in. The on'yomi is often used when a kanji combined with other components to form a word, as in "富士山 *Fujisan*".

Furthermore, in some cases a word will not use either the on'yomi or kun'yomi of its constituent kanji, but rather have its own special reading. For example, the first kanji in the word "今日" means "now" while the second means "day". When combined, the two are read as "きょう *kyo*" and represent "today". The sound "きょう *kyo*" has nothing to do with the readings of either kanji. It is only read that way to grasp the meaning. There are several such words within a typical working Japanese vocabulary.

4. Why are kanji used?

There are not any hard and fast rules about which words to use kanji with. It's more like a general set of standards. It is actually possible to write in Japanese without kanji and using only kana (hiragana and katakana) instead. In fact, that is how young children write. They gradually learn the kanji at school and become able to use more of them as they progress. However, not using kanji and only writing with kana makes sentences hard to understand. In addition, since Japanese does not have clear word units and there are no spaces placed between words, if you write only in kana then it is hard to know where the separators between meanings are. If you use kanji, on the other hand, then it becomes easier to perceive the sentence's structure and meaning.

In addition, Japanese has many homonyms (words with the same sounds), so kanji also help to differentiate between them.

In this textbook we use kanji that are often used in daily life, as well as for proper nouns, based on the N4 level of the Japanese-Language Proficiency Test.

5. Vertical and Horizontal Writing

Japanese can be written both vertically and horizontally. Newspapers are usually written vertically, as are many books and magazines, but the text may be printed with horizontal text depending on the content. Websites and emails are written horizontally. Printed material such as magazine covers can have both vertical and horizontal text.

III. Grammar
1. Basic Sentence Structure

Japanese generally has the below sort of structure in sentences containing a verb.

subject (S)	+	object (O)	+	verb (V)
わたし―は		カメラ―を		かいました。
Watashi-wa		kamera-o		kaimashita
I (subject/topic)		camera (object)		bought (verb)

The function of the subject, object and so on are not determined by their order in the sentence, but by the particles (the words in the boxes in the example above) that follow them. Nouns make no grammatical differentiation between singular and plural, gender or person, and they do not affect the form of the predicate. There are two different tenses: past and non-past (expressing both the present and future).

2. Word Order

The predicate (verbs, adjectives, the copula "です *desu*", etc.) comes last. As stated before, since a noun's function is indicated by a particle, you are allowed a relatively large amount of freedom to determine word order, but there are some limits, so you should begin by remembering the word order in the example sentences in this textbook as they appear here. The word order in all three of the sentences below is acceptable.

私は きのう 渋谷で カメラを 買いました。
Watashi wa kinō Shibuya de kamera o kaimashita.

きのう 私は 渋谷で カメラを 買いました。
Kinō watashi wa Shibuya de kamera o kaimashita.

渋谷で 私は きのうカメラを 買いました。
Shibuya de watashi wa kino kamera o kaimashita.

I bought a camera in Shibuya yesterday.

3. Types of Sentences

Generally speaking, Japanese has nominal sentences, adjectival sentences and verbal sentences. There are two kinds of adjectival sentences: the な ("na") adjectival sentence and the い ("i") adjectival sentence.

1. Nominal	クリスは学生です。	Chris is a student.
	Kurisu wa gakusei desu.	
2. na-adj.	クリスは元気です。	Chris is fine.
	Kurisu wa genki desu.	
3. i-adj.	すしはおいしいです。	Sushi is delicious.
	Sushi wa oishii desu.	
4. Verbal	クリスは映画を見ます。	Chris watches movies.
	Kurisu wa eiga o mimasu.	

*" です *desu*" comes at the end of nominal and adjectival sentences. The " ま す *masu*" at the end of a verbal sentence makes it formal and nonpast.

The possible conjugations for examples 1 through 4 above are given on p.97.

1. Nominal Sentences

	Affirmative	Negative
Nonpast	クリスは学生です。 Kurisu wa gakusei desu. Chris is a student.	クリスは学生じゃないです。 Kurisu wa gakusei janai desu. Chris is not a student.
Past	クリスは学生でした。 Kurisu wa gakusei deshita. Chris was a student.	クリスは学生じゃなかったです。 Kurisu wa gakusei janakatta desu. Chris was not a student.

2. Na-adjectival Sentences

▶See Unit 4

	Affirmative	Negative
Nonpast	クリスは元気です。 Kurisu wa genki desu. Chris is fine.	クリスは元気じゃないです。 Kurisu wa genki janai desu. Chris is not fine.
Past	クリスは元気でした。 Kurisu wa genki deshita. Chris was fine.	クリスは元気じゃなかったです。 Kurisu wa genki janakatta desu. Chris was not fine.

∗Nominal sentences and na-adjectival sentences have the same conjugations.

3. I-adjectival Sentences

▶See Unit 4

	Affirmative	Negative
Nonpast	すしはおいしいです。 Sushi wa oishii desu. Sushi is delicious.	すしはおいしくないです。 Sushi wa oishikunai desu. Sushi is not delicious.
Past	すしはおいしかったです。 Sushi wa oishikatta desu. Sushi was delicious.	すしはおいしくなかったです。 Sushi wa oishikunakatta desu. Sushi was not delicious.

4. Verbal Sentences

▶See Unit 1

	Affirmative	Negative
Nonpast	クリスは映画を見ます。 Kurisu wa eiga o mimasu. Chris watches movies.	クリスは映画を見ません。 Kurisu wa eiga o mimasen. Chris doesn't watch movies.
Past	クリスは映画を見ました。 Kurisu wa eiga o mimashita. Chris watched a movie.	クリスは映画を見ませんでした。 Kurisu wa eiga o mimasen deshita. Chris didn't watch a movie.

∗The nonpast form also represents the future.

クリスはあした映画を見ます。　　Chris will watch a movie tomorrow.
Kurisu wa ashita eiga o mimasu.

Distinctive Features of the Japanese Language ■ 97

4. Speech Styles 〈Formal and Informal Styles〉

Generally speaking, Japanese sentences have formal and informal styles. The formal style ends in " で す *desu*" or " ま す *masu*" , so it is also called the "desu-masu style" . The examples in the section "3. Types of Sentences" are all in the formal style.

Speaking in the informal style with a higher-ranking person, a business partner, a person you have just met and so on makes a rude impression, so you should be careful. On the other hand, if you always speak in the formal style with a friend you want to build familiarity with, it may be rather difficult to build up that familiarity. This textbook mostly uses the formal style, but there are also informal style sentences in conversations between friends and the like, so you can study both styles. You should go ahead and use the informal style while avoiding being rude to friends you want to build familiarity with.

Respectful words 〈honorific words and humble words〉 are also important components when it comes to speech styles. They are a very polite form of language used, for example, when you speak to a higher-ranking person or customer, or for speaking in formal settings. The words used by the restaurant staff in Unit 2 and the clerk in Unit 5, along with other places in this textbook, use some honorific words.

When written in the informal style, the example sentence types from the section "3. Types of Sentences" appear as below.

▶See Unit 1, 4 Notes

1. Nominal Sentences

	Affirmative	Negative
Nonpast	クリスは学生（だ）。 Kurisu wa gakusei (da). Chris is a student.	クリスは学生じゃない。 Kurisu wa gakusei janai. Chris is not a student.
Past	クリスは学生だった。 Kurisu wa gakusei datta. Chris was a student.	クリスは学生じゃなかった。 Kurisu wa gakusei janakatta. Chris was not a student.

2. Na-adjectival Sentences

	Affirmative	Negative
Nonpast	クリスは元気（だ）。 Kurisu wa genki (da). Chris is fine.	クリスは元気じゃない。 Kurisu wa genki janai. Chris is not fine.
Past	クリスは元気だった。 Kurisu wa genki datta. Chris was fine.	クリスは元気じゃなかった。 Kurisu wa genki janakatta. Chris was not fine.

＊Nominal sentences and na-adjectival sentences have the same conjugations.

3. I-adjectival Sentences

	Affirmative	Negative
Nonpast	すしはおいし<u>い</u>。 Sushi wa oishi<u>i</u>. Sushi is delicious.	すしはおいし<u>くない</u>。 Sushi wa oishi<u>kunai</u>. Sushi is not delicious.
Past	すしはおいし<u>かった</u>。 Sushi wa oishi<u>katta</u>. Sushi was delicious.	すしはおいし<u>くなかった</u>。 Sushi wa oishi<u>kunakatta</u>. Sushi was not delicious.

4. Verbal Sentences

	Affirmative	Negative
Nonpast	クリスは映画を見<u>る</u>。 Kurisu wa eiga o <u>miru</u>. Chris watches movies.	クリスは映画を見<u>ない</u>。 Kurisu wa eiga o <u>minai</u>. Chris doesn't watch movies.
Past	クリスは映画を見<u>た</u>。 Kurisu wa eiga o <u>mita</u>. Chris watched a movie.	クリスは映画を見<u>なかった</u>。 Kurisu wa eiga o <u>minakatta</u>. Chris didn't watch a movie.

＊The conjugations of informal style verbs vary according to the verb type. See the section "8. Verbs" for more information.

5. Interrogative Sentences

When using the formal style, adding "か ka" to the end of a sentence makes it an interrogative (question) sentence.

あした東京に行きます<u>か</u>。　Are you going to Tokyo tomorrow?
Ashita Tōkyō ni ikimasu <u>ka</u>.

When using the informal style, speaking with a rising intonation makes a sentence interrogative. We usually do not add "か ka" to the end.

あした東京に行く？　ノ　Are you going to Tokyo tomorrow?
Ashita Tōkyō ni iku?

In order to denote interrogative sentences in this book, a "？" is used at the end of these sentences in the informal style.

6. Omissions

When something is clear from the context, a word or phrase may be omitted. In addition, doing so makes your Japanese sound more natural.

A：(~~あなたは~~) 元気ですか。　How are you? / Are you alright?
　(~~Anata wa~~) genki desu ka.

B：はい。（私は）元気です。　Yes, I'm fine.

　　Hai. (~~watashi wa~~) genki desu.

▶See Unit 1 Notes

7. Particles

A particle comes after a noun and indicates the function of that noun within the sentence, such as subject or object. They are small yet important components. When a particle changes, it changes the meaning of the entire sentence.

友だちにプレゼントをもらいました。　My friend gave me a present.

　　Tomodachi ni purezento o moraimashita.

友だちはプレゼントをもらいました。　My friend received a present.

　　Tomodachi wa purezento o moraimashita.

Most particles can have multiple meanings and functions. The main particles and their meanings and functions are given below.

▶See Unit 1, 3, 4

は wa

〈topic〉　＊In many cases it represents the subject.

私はクリスです。　I'm Chris.

　　Watashi wa Kurisu desu.

今日はいそがしいです。　Today I'm busy.

　　Kyō wa isogasii desu.

〈compare & contrast〉

ねこは好きです。でも、いぬは好きじゃないです。　I like cats. But I don't like dogs.

　　Neko wa suki desu. Demo, inu wa suki janai desu.

を o

〈object〉

すしを食べます。　I eat sushi.

　　Sushi o tabemasu.

に ni

〈destination〉　＊ "へ" is also used this way.

東京に行きます。　I'm going to Tokyo.

　　Tōkyō ni ikimasu.

〈existing location〉

外にねこがいます。　There is a cat outside.

　　Soto ni neko ga imasu.

パソコンはここにあります。　There is a computer here.
　Pasokon wa koko ni arimasu.

⟨date & time⟩

6時に起きます。　I get up at six.
　Roku-ji ni okimasu.

1月15日にアメリカに帰ります。　I'm going to back to the USA on January 15th.
　Ichi-gatsu jūgo-nichi ni Amerika ni kaerimasu.

⟨person affected by the subject's action⟩

友だちに会います。　I'm going to see my friend.
　Tomodachi ni aimasu.

で de

⟨location of action⟩

うちで本を読みます。　I read books at home.
　Uchi de hon o yomimasu.

⟨method⟩

バスで大学に行きます。　I take the bus to university.
　Basu de daigaku ni ikimasu.

ペンで書きます。　I use a pen to write.
　Pen de kakimasu.

日本語で話します。　I speak in Japanese.
　Nihon-go de hanashimasu.

⟨scope⟩

和食で何が好きですか。　What Japanese foods do you like?
　Washoku de nani ga suki desu ka.

⟨selection⟩

これでいいです。　This is fine.
　Kore de ii desu.

と to

⟨noun and noun⟩

アニメとゲームが好きです。　I like anime and games.
　Anime to gemu ga suki desu.

⟨partner for an action⟩

えみさんと大阪に行きました。　I went to Osaka with Emi-san.
　Emi-san to Ōsaka ni ikimashita.

も mo

⟨also⟩

私<ruby>私<rt>わたし</rt></ruby>もアニメが好<ruby>好<rt>す</rt></ruby>きです。　I like anime too.

Watashi <u>mo</u> anime ga suki desu.

から kara

⟨starting point or departure point⟩

昼休<ruby>昼休<rt>ひるやす</rt></ruby>みは12時<ruby>時<rt>じ</rt></ruby>からです。　Lunch break is from 12:00.

Hiruyasumi wa jūni-ji <u>kara</u> desu.

東京<ruby>東京<rt>とうきょう</rt></ruby>からしんかんせんで大阪<ruby>大阪<rt>おおさか</rt></ruby>に行<ruby>行<rt>い</rt></ruby>きます。　I will take the bullet train from Tokyo to Osaka.

Tōkyō <u>kara</u> shinkansen de Ōsaka ni ikimasu.

まで made

⟨final location or time⟩

昼休<ruby>昼休<rt>ひるやす</rt></ruby>みは1時<ruby>時<rt>じ</rt></ruby>までです。　Lunch break lasts until 1:00.

Hiruyasumi wa ichi-ji <u>made</u> desu.

東京<ruby>東京<rt>とうきょう</rt></ruby>から大阪<ruby>大阪<rt>おおさか</rt></ruby>まで、しんかんせんで3時間<ruby>時間<rt>じかん</rt></ruby>ぐらいです。

Tōkyō kara Ōsaka <u>made</u>, shinkansen de san-jikan gurai desu.

It takes about three hours by bullet train from Tokyo to Osaka.

より yori

⟨object of comparison⟩

しんかんせんはバスよりはやいです。　The bullet train is faster than the bus.

Shinkansen wa basu <u>yori</u> hayai desu.

の no

1. Connects a noun with another noun and represents various meanings.

⟨possession⟩

これは私<ruby>私<rt>わたし</rt></ruby>の本<ruby>本<rt>ほん</rt></ruby>です。　This is my bus.

Kore wa watashi <u>no</u> hon desu.

⟨affiliation⟩

クリスはテキサス大学<ruby>大学<rt>だいがく</rt></ruby>の学生<ruby>学生<rt>がくせい</rt></ruby>です。　Chris is a student at the University of Texas.

Kurisu wa Tekisasu daigaku <u>no</u> gakusei desu.

⟨properties, types⟩

日本<ruby>日本<rt>にほん</rt></ruby>の音楽<ruby>音楽<rt>おんがく</rt></ruby>が好<ruby>好<rt>す</rt></ruby>きです。　I like Japanese music.

Nihon <u>no</u> ongaku ga suki desu.

2. Can also be used to make pronouns.

これは私のです。　This is mine.

Kore wa watashi <u>no</u> desu.

"が *ga*" is principally used in certain sentence structures or situations. "は *wa*" and "が *ga*" are interchangeable at times, but since the differences between the two are very complex, for now you should just know that "が *ga*" is used in the following cases.

1. Object of a specific predicate

（私は）アニメが好きです。　I like anime.

(Watashi wa) anime <u>ga</u> <u>suki</u> desu.

（私は）うたが上手です。　I'm good at singing.

(Watashi wa) uta <u>ga</u> <u>jōzu</u> desu.

（私は）じゅうどうができます。　I can do judo.

(Watashi wa) jūdō <u>ga</u> <u>dekimasu</u>.

お金があります。／ねこがいます。　I have money. / There is a cat.

O-kane <u>ga</u> <u>arimasu</u>. / Neko <u>ga</u> <u>imasu</u>.

2. Expresses an aspect of the subject

えみはかみが長いです。　Emi has long hair.

Emi wa <u>kami ga nagai</u> desu.

東京は人が多いです。　There are lots of people in Tokyo.

Tōkyō wa <u>hito ga ōi</u> desu.

3. If the subject is a question word

だれが来ますか。　Who is coming?

<u>Dare ga</u> kimasu ka.

いつがいいですか。　When is best for you?

<u>Itsu ga</u> ii desu ka.

8. Verbs

1. Groups

Verbs are categorized into three types according to how they are conjugated.

Group	Examples	
Ⅰ　(u-verb)	行く iku (go)	飲む nom<u>u</u> (drink)
Ⅱ　(ru-verb)	食べる taber<u>u</u> (eat)	見る mir<u>u</u> (look)
Ⅲ　(irregular verb)	する suru (do)	来る kuru (come)

＊These are the only two verbs in this group.

＊There are some u-verbs that end in "る *ru*" ("帰る *kaeru*", "切る *kiru*", "入る *hairu*", etc.).

2. Conjugations

There are many conjugated forms for verbs. The main conjugated forms are below. See the supplementary volume for the conjugated forms of each verb.

Masu-form   E.g. 食べ（ます）　tabe（masu）

This is primarily used at the end of a sentence in the formal style. Using only the masu-form, you can combine it with verb stems to make affirmative, negative, nonpast and past verb tenses in the formal style. Refer to the section "3. Types of Sentences" .

クリスはすしを　　食べます／食べません／食べました／食べませんでした。

Kurisu wa sushi o　tabemasu / tabemasen / tabemashita / tabemasen deshita.

In this book, we only call the "食べ *tabe*" part of the verb "食べる *taberu*" the "masu-form" .

You can also use it in the following kinds of sentence patterns.

すしが食べたいです。　I want to eat sushi.

Sushi ga tabetai desu.　　　　　　　　　　　　　　　　　▶See Unit 4

いっしょに昼ご飯を食べませんか。　Let's have lunch.

Issho ni hirugohan o tabemasen ka.　　　　　　　　　▶See Extra Lesson 1

パーティーに行きましょう。　Let's go to the party.

Pathī ni ikimasho.

Dictionary form   E.g. 食べる　taberu

This is the basic verb form. When you look for a verb in the dictionary, look for this form. It is used at the end of a sentence in the informal style to represent the nonpast and affirmation.

クリスはすしを食べる。

Kurisu wa sushi o taberu.

This form can also be used in the middle of a sentence, as in the following sentence patterns.

本を読むことが好きです。　I like to read books.

Hon o yomu koto ga suki desu.　　　　　　　　　　　▶See Unit 1

しゅみは本を読むことです。　Reading books is one of the things I like to do.

Shumi wa hon o yomu koto desu.

日本語の本を読むことができます。　I can read Japanese books.

Nihon-go no hon o yomu koto ga dekimasu.　　　　　▶See Unit 4

ご飯を食べるとき、はしを使います。　I use chopsticks when I eat.

Gohan o taberu toki, hashi o tsukaimasu.　　　　　　▶See Unit 6

Ta-form   E.g. 食べた　tabeta

This form is used at the end of a sentence in the informal style to represent the past and affirmation. (For group I verbs, there are some conjugation patterns.)

クリスはすしを食べた。

Kurisu wa sushi o tabeta.

This form can also be used in the middle of a sentence, as in the following sentence patterns.

大阪に行ったことがあります。 I have been to Osaka.

Ōsaka ni itta koto ga arimasu. ▶See Unit 6

大学が終わったら、また日本に来たいです。

Daigaku ga owattara, mata Nihon ni kitai desu. ▶See Unit 6

I want to come to Japan again after I graduate from university.

大阪に行ったとき、大阪城を見ました。 When I went to Osaka, I visited Osaka Castle.

Ōsaka ni itta toki, Ōsakajō o mimashita. ▶See Unit 6

| Te-form | E.g. 食べて　tabete

With this form you can connect a variety of components to make sentence patterns. It is used in the following kinds of sentence patterns (with the same conjugation rules as the ta-form above).

食べてください。／食べて。 Please eat. / Eat.

Tabete kudasai. / Tabete. ▶See Unit 3

ごはんを食べて、テレビを見て、ねました。 I had a meal, watched TV, and then went to bed.

Gohano tabete, terebi o mite, nemashita. ▶See Unit 4

トイレに行ってもいいですか。 May I go to the restroom?

Toire ni ittemo ii desu ka.

おいしいご飯を作ってくれて、ありがとうございました。

Oishii gohan o tsukutte kurete, arigatō gozaimashita. ▶See Unit 6

Thank you for making delicious meals.

| Nai-form | E.g. 食べない　tabenai

This form is mostly used at the end of a sentence in the informal style to express negation and the nonpast.

クリスはすしを食べない。

Kurisu wa sushi o tabenai.

It can also be used in the following kinds of sentence patterns.

ここで食べないでください。 Please don't eat here.

Koko de tabenaide kudasai.

勉強しなければなりません。 I have to study.

Benkyō shinakereba narimasen. ▶See Unit 6

しゅくだいをしなくてもいいです。 You don't have to do any homework.

Shukudai o shinakutemo ii desu.

| Volitional form | E.g. 食べよう　tabeyō

This form is mostly used at the end of a sentence in the informl style to express an invitation or intention.

パーティーに行こう。　Let's go to the party.

　Pāthī ni ikō.

いっしょに昼ご飯を食べよう。　Let's have lunch together.

　Issho ni hirugohan o tabeyō.

It can also be used in the following kinds of sentence patterns.

また日本に来ようと思います。　I would like to come to Japan again in the future.

　Mata Nihon ni koyō to omoimasu.

Potential form　　E.g. 食べられる　taberareru

This form expresses a person's abilities or situational potential.

私はさしみが食べられます。　I can eat sashimi.

　Watashi wa sashimi ga taberaremasu.

学生は大学の図書館が使えます。　Students can use the university library.

　Gakusei wa daigaku no toshokan ga tsukaemasu.

9. Adjectives

There are two groups of adjectives (na-adjectives and i-adjectives).

Group	Examples
na-adjective	元気 genki　しずか shizuka　きれい kirei*　好き suki
i-adjective	大きい ōkii　高い takai　かわいい kawaii　たのしい tanoshii

＊Some na-adjectives also end in "い *i*" ("きれい *kirei*", "きらい *kirai*", "有名 *yūmei*", etc.).

Refer to the section "3. Types of Sentences" for conjugating when the predicate is an adjective. The following conjugations are used when two or more adjectives are connected.

[na-adjective]

クリスは元気で、やさしいです。　Chris is an active and kind person.

　Kurisu wa genki de, yasashii desu.

[i-adjective]

ラーメンはおいしくて、安いです。　Ramen is delicious and cheap.

　Rāmen wa oishikute, yasui desu.

The adjectives are used as below when modifying a noun.

[na-adjective]

元気な人　genki na hito　　healthy (active) person

好きな音楽　suki na ongaku　　favorite music

[i-adjective]

おいしいすし　oishii sushi　　delicious sushi

白いねこ　shiroi neko　　a white cat

▶See Unit 4

106

Answer Keys and CD Script

Unit 1

Exercise 1

Ex. こんにちは。クリスです。アメリカから来ました。大学生です。アニメが好きです。よろしくお願いします。

> Konnichiwa. Kurisu desu. Amerika kara kimashita. Daigakusei desu. Anime ga suki desu. Yoroshiku onegaishimasu.

> Hi, I'm Chris. I came from the U.S. I'm a college student. I like anime. Nice to meet you.

1. シンです。はじめまして。**台湾**から来ました。**会社員**です。**映画が好きです。**日本の映画をよく見ます。よろしくお願いします。

> Shin desu. Hajimemashite. **Taiwan** kara kimashita. **Kaishain** desu. **Eiga ga suki desu.** Nihon no eiga o yoku mimasu. Yoroshiku onegaishimasu.

> Hello, my name is Xin. I'm from Taiwan. I'm a company employee. I like movies. I often watch Japanese movies. Nice to meet you.

2. こんにちは。カルロスです。**ブラジル**から来ました。**エンジニア**です。**しゅみは料理です。**よろしくお願いします。

> Konnichiwa. Karurosu desu. **Burajiru** kara kimashita. **Enjinia** desu. **Shumi wa ryōri desu.** Yoroshiku onegaishimasu.

> Hi, I'm Carlos. I'm from Brazil. I'm an engineer. I enjoy cooking. Nice to meet you.

3. はじめまして。アートです。しゅっしんは**タイ**です。**きょうし**です。**本が好きです。**日本の本も好きです。よろしくお願いします。

> Hajimemashite. Āto desu. Shusshin wa **Tai** desu. **Kyōshi** desu. **Hon ga suki desu.** Nihon no hon mo suki desu. Yoroshiku onegaishimasu.

> Hello. Please call me Art. I'm from Thailand. I'm a teacher. I like books. I also like Japanese books. Nice to meet you.

Unit 2

Exercise 1

Ⅰ

Ex. A：何名様ですか。

> Nan-mei-sama desu ka.
> How many people?

B：3人です。　San-nin desu.　Three.

1. A：何名様ですか。

> Nan-mei-sama desu ka.
> How many people?

B：2人です。　Futari desu.　Two.

2. A：何名様ですか。

> Nan-mei-sama desu ka.
> How many people?

B：7人です。　Shichi-nin desu. Seven.

3. A：何名様ですか。

> Nan-mei-sama desu ka.
> How many people?

B：9人です。　Kyū-nin desu.　Nine.

4. A：何名様ですか。

> Nan-mei-sama desu ka.
> How many people?

B：4人です。　Yo-nin desu.　Four.

5. A：何名様ですか。

> Nan-mei-sama desu ka.
> How many people?

B：1人です。　Hitori desu.　One.

6. A：何名様ですか。

> Nan-mei-sama desu ka.
> How many people?

B：6人です。　Roku-nin desu.　Six.

Ⅱ

Ex. A：いくつですか。　Ikutsu desu ka.

> How many?

B：2つです。　Futatsu desu.　Two.

1. A：いくつですか。　Ikutsu desu ka.

> How many?

B：4つです。　Yottsu desu.　Four.

2. A：いくつですか。　Ikutsu desu ka.

> How many?

B：5つです。　Itsutsu desu.　Five.

3. A：いくつですか。　Ikutsu desu ka.

> How many?

B：8つです。　Yattsu desu.　Eight.

4. A：いくつですか。　Ikutsu desu ka.

> How many?

B：3つです。 Mittsu desu. Three.

5. A：いくつですか。 Ikutsu desu ka.
      How many?

   B：9つです。 Kokonotsu desu.
      Nine.

6. A：いくつですか。 Ikutsu desu ka.
      How many?

   B：1つです。 Hitotsu desu. One.

Ⅲ

Ex. A：これはいくらですか。
      Kore wa ikura desu ka.
      How much is this?

   B：150円です。 Hyaku gojū-en desu.
      It's 150 yen.

1. A：これはいくらですか。
      Kore wa ikura desu ka.
      How much is this?

   B：2,000円です。 Nisen-en desu.
      It's 2000 yen.

2. A：これはいくらですか。
      Kore wa ikura desu ka.
      How much is this?

   B：175円です。
      Hyaku nanajū go-en desu.
      It's 175 yen.

3. A：これはいくらですか。
      Kore wa ikura desu ka.
      How much is this?

   B：98円です。
      Kyūjū hachi-en desu. It's 98 yen.

4. A：これはいくらですか。
      Kore wa ikura desu ka.
      How much is this?

   B：6,490円です。
      Rokusen yonhyaku kyūjū-en desu.
      It's 6,490 yen.

5. A：これはいくらですか。
      Kore wa ikura desu ka.
      How much is this?

   B：37,000円です。
      Sanman nanasen-en desu.
      It's 37,000 yen.

6. A：これはいくらですか。

Kore wa ikura desu ka.
How much is this?

   B：1,840円です。
      Sen happyaku yonjū-en desu.
      It's 1,840 yen.

7. コーヒーは150円です。サンドイッチは300円です。
      Kōhī wa hyaku gojū-en desu. Sandoicchi wa sanbyaku-en desu.
      Coffee is 150 yen. Sandwich is 300 yen.

   コーヒー1つ、サンドイッチ1つ、お願いします。いくらですか。
      Kōhī hitotsu, sandoicchi hitotsu, onegaishimasu. Ikura desu ka.
      One coffee and one sandwich, please. How much are these?

   Answer: 450 yen

Unit 3

Exercise 1

Ex. c A：こんにちは、おじゃまします。
       Konnichiwa, ojamashimasu.

    B：こんにちは。どうぞ、こちらへ。
       Konnichiwa. Dōzo, kochira e.

    A：Hello, may I come in?

    B：Hello. Please, right this way.

1. a A：すみません、あのケーキはいくらですか。
       Sumimasen, ano kēki wa ikura desu ka.

    B：2,000円です。 Nisen-en desu.

    A：Excuse me, how much is that cake?

    B：It's 2,000 yen.

2. f A：それはクリスさんの本ですか。
       Sore wa Kurisu-san no hon desu ka.

    B：いいえ、私のじゃないです。
       Iie, watashi no janai desu.

    A：Is this yours Chris?

    B：No, it's not mine.

3. e A：この漢字を読んでください。
       Kono kanji o yonde kudasai.

    B：わかりません。
       Wakarimasen.

A：Please read this kanji.

B：Sorry, I don't know how (to read it).

4. **d** A：これ、だれのかさ？

   Kore, dare no kasa?

  B：あ、それ、私の。

   A, sore, watashi no.

  A：Whose is this?

  B：Ah, that's mine.

5. **b** A：あそこにえみがいる！　3人でいっしょに帰らない？

   Asoko ni Emi ga iru! San-nin de issho ni kaeranai?

  B：うん！

   Un!

  A：Emi's over there! Should the three of us go together?

  B：Sure!

Exercise 2

1. この絵を**見てください**。
 Kono e o **mite kudasai.**
2. 電気を**消してください**。
 Denki o **keshite kudasai.**
3. 毎日**勉強してください**。
 Mainichi **benkyō shite kudasai.**
4. どうぞ、コーヒーを**飲んでください**。
 Dōzo, kōhi o **nonde kudasai.**
5. ちょっと**待ってください**。
 Chotto **matte kudasai.**
6. どうぞ、**すわってください**。
 Dōzo, **suwatte kudasai.**
7. ここに名前を**書いてください**。
 Koko ni namae o **kaite kudasai.**

Unit 4

Exercise 1

Ex. **d** 寒いです。　Samui desu.　It's cold.

1. **c** むずかしいです。　Muzukashii desu.
  It's difficult.

2. **h** こわい。　Kowai.　It's scary.

3. **f** うるさい。　Urusai.　It's noisy.

4. **b** 暑いです。　Atsui desu.　It's hot.

5. **a** 上手です。　Jōzu desu.　She is good.

6. **e** きれいじゃないです。
  Kirei janai desu.
  It's not clean.

7. **g** ぜんぜんひまじゃない。
  Zenzen hima janai.
  I'm not free at all.

Unit 5

Exercise 1

Ex. **a** A：あのー、写真、いいですか。

   Anō, shashin, ii desu ka.

  B：あ、どうぞ。

   A, dōzo.

  A：Excuse me, sir. May I take some photos?

  B：Go ahead.

1. **a** A：先生、じしょ、いいですか。

   Sensei, jisho, ii desu ka.

  B：いいえ、じしょは使いません。

   Iie, jisho wa tsukaimasen.

  A：わかりました。

   Wakarimashita.

  A：Ma'am. May I use a dictionary?

  B：No, you may not.

  A：Ok, I understand.

2. **b** A：クリス、今日カラオケに行かない？

   Kurisu, kyō karaokae ni ikanai?

  B：んー、ごめんね。今日はちょっと…。

   Nn, gomenne. Kyō wa chotto...

  A：じゃあ、またね。

   Jā, matane.

  A：Chris, do you want to go to karaoke today?

  B：Hmm, today is no good for me...

  A：OK, another time then.

3. **b** A：ここ、いいですか。

   Koko, ii desu ka.

  B：あ、ここ、います。

   A, koko, imasu.

A：Excuse me. May I sit here?

B：Ah, sorry. This seat is taken.

4. **a** A：すみません。スーパーはどこですか。

    Sumimasen, sūpā wa doko desu ka.

B：その角を右に曲がって、まっすぐ行ってください。右にあります。

    Sono kado o migi ni magatte, massugu itte kudasai. Migi ni arimasu.

A：Excuse me. Where is the supermarket?

B：Turn right at the corner, and then go straight. It's on the right.

Exercise 2（example answer）

1. しお、**いいですか。**／しお、**お願いします。**／しおを**取ってください。**

    Shio, **ii desu ka.** / Shio, **onegaishimasu.** / Shio **o totte kudasai.**

2. このCDを**聞きたいんですが…。**

    Kono CD o **kikitai n desu ga...**

3. あした、**いいですか。**

    Ashita, **ii desu ka.**

4. ごめんね。**あしたはちょっと…。**／テニスは**ちょっと…。**

    Gomenne. **Ahita wa chotto... / Tenisu wa chotto...**

5. 旅行にもうしこみたいんですが…。

    Ryokō ni mōshikomitai n desu ga...

6. どうやって使いますか。

    Dōyatte tsukaimasu ka.

Unit 6

Exercise 1

1. クリスです。日本はとても楽しかったです。たくさん友だちを作りました。…大学をそつぎょうしたら、また日本に来て、日本ではたらきたいです。

    Kurisu desu. Nihon wa totemo tanoshikatta desu. **Takusan tomodachi o tsukurimashita.** ... **Daigaku o sotsugyō shitara, mata Nihon ni kite, Nihon de hatarakitai desu.**

    I'm Chris. Japan was so much fun. I made a lot of friends. ... After graduating from college, I want to come back to Japan and find a job.

2. シンです。日本の生活は楽しかったです。**たくさん旅行しました。**でも、今、台湾に帰りたいです。…**しょうらいは、まだわかりません。**

    Shin desu. Nihon no seikatsu wa tanoshikatta desu. **Takusan ryokō shimashita.** Demo, ima, Taiwan ni kaeritai desu. ... **Shōrai wa, mada wakarimasen.**

    I'm Xin. I had fun living in Japan. I traveled a lot. But, now, I feel like going back to Taiwan. ... I don't have any plans for the future right now.

3. カルロスです。日本語はむずかしかったです。でも、クラスの友だちといっしょに勉強しました。今、大丈夫です。…これからブラジルに帰って、日本の会社ではたらきます。また日本に来たいです。

    Karurosu desu. **Nihon-go wa muzukashikatta desu. Demo, kurasu no tomodachi to issho ni benkyō shimashita.** Ima, daijōbu desu. ... **Korekara Burajiru ni kaette, Nihon no kaisha de hatarakimasu.** Mata Nihon ni kitai desu.

    I'm Carlos. Japanese was difficult. But, I studied together with my friends in class. Now, I can speak the language fairly well. ... I'll go back to Brazil and work for a Japanese company. I want to come back to Japan some time in the future.

4. アートです。日本の食べ物はおいしいです。たくさん食べました。…私はしょうらい、日本の大学でタイ語を教えたいです。だから、これからも日本語を勉強します。がんばります。

    Āto desu. **Nihon no tabemono wa oishii desu. Takusan tabemashita.** ... **Watashi wa shōrai, Nihon no daigaku de Tai-go o oshietai desu.** Dakara, korekara mo Nihon-go o benkyō shimasu. Ganbarimasu.

    I'm Art. Japanese food is delicious. I ate a lot. ... In the future, I want to teach Thai at a university in Japan. So, I'll continue studying Japanese. I'll give it my best.

Index

著者　　上原 由美子（うえはら ゆみこ）
　　　　神田外語大学留学生別科専任講師

　　　　菊池 民子（きくち たみこ）
　　　　元神田外語大学留学生別科専任講師、中国帰国者支援・交流センター非常勤講師

翻訳	株式会社ラテックス・インターナショナル
DTP	株式会社明昌堂
イラスト	パント大吉
カバーデザイン	岡崎裕樹（アスク出版）
ナレーション	江尻拓己、神田和佳
録音・編集	スタジオ グラッド

NIHONGO ACTIVE TALK
The First Japanese Textbook for Beginners

2014年7月31日　初版　第1刷発行

発行人	天谷修平
発行	株式会社アスク出版
	〒162-8558　東京都新宿区下宮比町2-6
	TEL 03-3267-6864　FAX 03-3267-6867　http://www.ask-books.com/
印刷・製本	株式会社光邦

Vocabulary List

Words and Phrases for Unit 1-6

Unit 1

Nouns

（お）名前	(o)namae	name

*The prefix "o-" and "go-" makes nouns more polite.

アメリカ	Amerika	U.S.
しゅみ	shumi	hobby, interest
アニメ	anime	cartoons, anime
日本	Nihon	Japan
音楽	ongaku	music
私	watashi	I, me
（メール）アドレス	(mēru)adoresu	(e-mail)address
学生	gakusei	student
映画	eiga	movie
買い物	kaimono	shopping
しゅっしん	shusshin	birthplace, hometown
日本語	Nihon-go	Japanese(language)
Jポップ	J-poppu	J-pop
本	hon	book
すし	sushi	sushi
大学生	daigakusei	university student
スポーツ	supōtsu	sport
台湾	Taiwan	Taiwan
会社員	kaishain	company employee
ブラジル	Burajiru	Brazil
エンジニア	enjinia	engineer
料理	ryōri	dish
タイ	Tai	Thailand
教師	kyōshi	teacher
コーヒー	kōhī	coffee
サッカー	sakkā	soccer, football
ギター	gitā	guitar

Verbs   masu-form / dictionary form(group Ⅰ, Ⅱ, Ⅲ)

来ます／来る（Ⅲ）	kimasu / kuru	come
見ます／見る（Ⅱ）	mimasu / miru	look; see; watch
聞きます／聞く（Ⅰ）	kikimasu / kiku	listen; hear
メールします／メールする（Ⅲ）	mēru shimasu / mēru suru	send e-mail
行きます／行く（Ⅰ）	ikimasu / iku	go
します／する（Ⅲ）	shimasu / suru	do
勉強します／勉強する（Ⅲ）	benkyō shimasu / benkyō suru	study
読みます／読む（Ⅰ）	yomimasu / yomu	read
食べます／食べる（Ⅱ）	tabemasu / taberu	eat
飲みます／飲む（Ⅰ）	nomimasu / nomu	drink
（ギターを）ひきます／ひく（Ⅰ）	(gitā o)hikimasu / hiku	play(guitar)

Adjectives

好き（な）	suki(na)	like

Adverbs & Others

うん。	Un.	Yes.(casual)
～さん	-san	Mr. / Mrs. / Miss. / Ms. (a form of address that follows a name)
よく	yoku	frequently, often
これ	kore	this
あした	ashita	tomorrow
きのう	kinō	yesterday
毎日	mainichi	every day
ときどき	tokidoki	sometimes
あまり	amari	(not)really
ぜんぜん	zenzen	never,(not)at all
ううん。	Uun.	No.(casual)

Unit 2

Nouns

（お）たばこ	(o)tabako	cigarrettes
きんえん	kin'en	non-smoking
きつえん	kitsuen	smoking
（ご）注文	(go)chūmon	order
サンドイッチ	sandoicchi	sandwich
ハンバーグ	hanbāgu	hamburg steak
定食	teishoku	set meal
（お）飲み物	(o)nomimono	drink
ハンバーガー	hanbāgā	hamburger
メニュー	menyū	menu
英語	Eigo	English(language)
トイレ	toire	toilet, bathroom
（お）酒	(o)sake	alcohol; liquor

パーティー	pāthī	party
日本料理 (にほんりょうり)	Nihon-ryōri	Japanese food
レストラン	resutoran	restaurant
昼ご飯 (ひるはん)	hirugohan	lunch
食べ物 (たもの)	tabemono	food
スプーン	supūn	spoon

Verbs

あります／ある（Ⅰ）	arimasu / aru	be(thing)
います／いる（Ⅱ）	imasu / iru	be(person, animal)
ちがいます／ちがう（Ⅰ） chigaimasu / chigau		be different

Adjectives

| おいしい | oishii | good, delicious, yummy |
| 新しい (あたらしい) | atarashii | new |

Adverbs & Others

～名様 (めいさま)	-mei-sama ～people(polite counter suffix for people)	
あとで	atode	later
あのー	anō	excuse me
まだ	mada	not～yet
すぐに	suguni	immediately
べつべつに	betsubetsuni	separately
～円 (えん)	en	yen
たくさん	takusan	a lot
いっぱい	ippai	a lot; full(casual)
少し (すこし)	sukoshi	a little
ちょっと	chotto	a little(casual)

Extra Lesson 1

Nouns

（お）まつり	(o)matsuri	festival
ねこカフェ	neko-kafe	cat cafe
テスト	tesuto	test, exam
日 (ひ)	hi	day; date
ご飯 (はん)	gohan	meal; lunch
ピザ	piza	pizza

Adjectives

| ひま（な） | hima(na) | free |

Adverbs & Others

| 来週 (らいしゅう) | raishū | next week |

いっしょに	issho ni	together
いい（です）ね。	Ii(desu)ne.	That sounds good.
いつ	itsu	when
～日 (にち)	-nichi	～th (date)
日曜日 (にちようび)	nichiyōbi	Sunday
土曜日 (どようび)	doyōbi	Saturday
月曜日 (げつようび)	getsuyōbi	Monday
じゃあ	jā	well then
ほか（の）	hoka(no)	other
たぶん	tabun	perhaps
今日 (きょう)	kyō	today

Unit 3

Nouns

パソコン	pasokon	personal computer
かばん	kaban	bag
漢字 (かんじ)	kanji	Chinese characters
時間 (じかん)	jikan	time
歌手 (かしゅ)	kashu	singer
人 (ひと)	hito	people, person
ケーキ	kēki	cake
かさ	kasa	umbrella
絵 (え)	e	picture
電気 (でんき)	denki	electricity; light
週末 (しゅうまつ)	shūmatsu	weekend
予定 (よてい)	yotei	schedule
意味 (いみ)	imi	meaning
例文 (れいぶん)	reibun	example sentence
辞書 (じしょ)	jisho	dictionary
図書館 (としょかん)	toshokan	library

Verbs

教えます／教える（Ⅱ） oshiemasu / oshieru		tell
使います／使う（Ⅰ） tsukaimasu / tsukau		use
入れます／入れる（Ⅱ） iremasu / ireru		enter; put in
すわります／すわる（Ⅰ） suwarimasu / suwaru		sit
作ります／作る（Ⅰ） tsukurimasu / tsukuru		make
待ちます／待つ（Ⅰ） machimasu / matsu		wait
わかります／わかる（Ⅰ） wakarimasu / wakaru		understand

3

帰ります／帰る（Ⅰ） kaerimasu / kaeru		return
起きます／起きる（Ⅱ） okimasu / okiru		get up
消します／消す（Ⅰ） keshimasu / kesu		turn off
書きます／書く（Ⅰ） kakimasu / kaku		write
入ります／入る（Ⅰ） hairimasu / hairu		enter
びっくりします／びっくりする（Ⅲ） bikkuri shimasu / bikkuri suru		be surprised

Adverbs & Others

おじゃまします。 Ojamashimasu.	Pardon the intrusion; Excuse me (greeting used when entering someone's office or home)	
ちょっと	chotto	a little
どうも	dōmo	somehow, likely
どうぞ Dōzo.	Go ahead; please(used to encourage, not to make a request)	
もう一度	mō ichido	once again
ごめん。	Gomen.	I'm sorry.
そうです。	Sō desu.	That's right.
いっしょに	isshoni	together

Extra Lesson 2
Nouns

イギリス	Igirisu	United Kingdom
フランス	Furansu	France
男の人	otoko-no-hito	man
中学校	chūgakkō	junior high school
先生	sensei	teacher
女の子	onna-no-ko	girl
小学生	shōgakusei primary school student	
家族	kazoku	family
写真	shashin	photo
ぼく boku	I, me(casual form of "watashi" that boys often use)	

Adjectives

（背が）高い	(se ga)takai	(tall)high
きれい（な）	kirei(na)	pretty
かわいい	kawaii	cute
わかい	wakai	young
かっこいい	kakkoii	good-looking

Adverbs & Others

～さい	-sai	～ years old
今	ima	now
ふーん。	Fūn.	Hmm.
そっくり	sokkuri	look like

Unit 4
Nouns

ホストファミリー	hosutofamirī	host family
おみやげ	omiyage	souvenirs
大阪城	Ōsakajō	Osaka castle
町	machi	town
しんかんせん	shinkansen	bullet train
バス	basu	bus
ラーメン	rāmen	ramen
Tシャツ	thīshatsu	t-shirt
スーパー	sūpā	supermarket
ホテル	hoteru	hotel
ひこうき	hikōki	airplane
サーフィン	sāfin	surfing
生活	seikatsu	life
私たち	watashitachi	we, us
写真	shashin	photo
たこやき	takoyaki	takoyaki
旅行	ryokō	travel; trip
質問	shitsumon	question

Verbs

かかります／かかる（Ⅰ） kakarimasu / kakaru		it takes(time)
買います／買う（Ⅰ）	kaimasu / kau	buy

Adjectives

楽しい	tanoshii	fun
高い	takai	high; expensive
安い	yasui	cheap
おそい	osoi	slow
大好き（な）	daisuki(na)	love
元気（な）	genki(na)	healthy; happy
親切（な）	shinsetsu(na)	helpful
かっこいい	kakkoii	cool
上手（な）	jōzu(na)	good
暑い	atsui	hot
むずかしい	muzukashii	difficult

寒い	samui	cold
きれい（な）	kirei(na)	clean
うるさい	urusai	noisy
ひま（な）	hima(na)	free
こわい	kowai	scary
大きい	ōkii	large

Adverbs & Others

先週	senshū	last week
とても	totemo	very
まず	mazu	first
それから	sorekara	then
～ぐらい	～ gurai	about ～
～時間	-jikan	～ hour
また	mata	again
まあまあ	māmā	so so
午前/午後～時	gozen / gogo -ji	am/pm o'clock
歩いて	aruite	on foot
でも	demo	but
だから	dakara	so
一番	ichiban	most
週末	shūmatsu	weekend
以上です。	ijō desu.	that's all.

Extra Lesson 3

Verbs

ねます／ねる（Ⅱ）	nemasu / neru	go to bed; sleep

Adverbs & Others

どうしましたか。	Dōshimashita ka.	What's happened?
1日3回	ichi-nichi san-kai	three times a day
早く	hayaku	early
お大事に。	Odaijini.	Take care of yourself.

Unit 5

Nouns

シャツ	shatsu	shirt
しちゃく	shichaku	try
水	mizu	water
ボタン	botan	button
ゆうびんきょく	yūbinkyoku	postal bureau
建物	tatemono	building
銀行	ginkō	bank
かど	kado	excess

テスト	tesuto	test
ねだん	nedan	price
ふくろ	fukuro	return path
（お）はし	(o)hashi	chopsticks
カラオケ	karaoke	karaoke
しお	shio	salt
しゅくだい	shukudai	homework
テニス	tenisu	tennis
電車	densha	electric train
サイズ	saizu	size

Verbs

聞きます／聞く（Ⅰ） kikimasu / kiku	ask
まがります／まがる（Ⅰ） magarimasu / magaru	turn
あたためます／あたためる（Ⅱ） atatamemasu / atatameru	warm
いります／いる（Ⅰ） irimasu / iru	need
わすれます／わすれる（Ⅱ） wasuremasu / wasureru	forget
もうしこみます／もうしこむ（Ⅰ） mōshikomimasu / mōshikomu	apply for; sign up
かんがえます／かんがえる（Ⅱ） kangaemasu / kangaeru	think

Adjectives

白い	shiroi	white
小さい	chiisai	small

Adverbs & Others

～番	-ban	Number. ～
ちょうど	chōdo	just
まっすぐ	massugu	straight
右	migi	right
左	hidari	left
～つめ	-tsume	～ th(second, third, fourth, etc.)
今度	kondo	now; next time
同じ	onaji	same
最近	saikin	recently
～線	-sen	～ line
～駅	-eki	～ station
～だけ	～ dake	only ～

Unit 6

Nouns

クラス	kurasu	class
友だち	tomodachi	friend
けいけん	keiken	experience
夏	natsu	summer
大学	daigaku	university
きかい	kikai	chance
エアコン	eakon	air conditioning
子ども	kodomo	child, children
まんが	manga	manga
夏休み	natsuyasumi	summer vacation
アルバイト	arubaito	part-time job
国	kuni	country, home country
しょうらい	shōrai	future
サムライ	samurai	samurai
ロールプレイングゲーム rōru-pureingu-gēmu		role-playing game
こと	koto	thing

Verbs

がんばります／がんばる（I） ganbarimasu / ganbaru		do one's best; work hard
そつぎょうします／そつぎょうする（III） sotsugyō shimasu / sotsugyō suru		graduate
はたらきます／はたらく（I） hatarakimasu / hataraku		work
てつだいます／てつだう（I） tetsudaimasu / tetsudau		help
れんらくします／れんらくする（III） renraku shimasu / renraku suru		contact
なります／なる（I）　narimasu / naru		become
思います／思う（I） omoimasu / omou		think

Adjectives

いい	ii	good

*The past tense of "ii" is "yokatta".

すごい	sugoi	amazing
おもしろい	omoshiroi	funny

Adverbs & Others

来週	raishū	next week
日曜日	nichiyōbi	Sunday
大丈夫	daijōbu	all right
いろいろ	iroiro	various
これからも	korekara mo	in the future
（お）元気で。	(O)genki de.	Take care.
そして	soshite	and
来年	rainen	next year
もう	mō	already
まだ	mada	yet
本当（に）	hontō ni	really
～家	-ke	～ family
みなさん	minasan	you all
～か月間	-kagetsukan	～ months

Useful Words by Category

Countries and Regions
国と地域　くにとちいき　Kuni to Chiiki

North / Centarl / South America

アメリカ	Amerika	The United States of America
アルゼンチン	Aruzenchin	Argentina
カナダ	Kanada	Canada
コロンビア	Koronbia	Colombia
ブラジル	Burajiru	Brazil
ペルー	Perū	Peru
メキシコ	Mekishiko	Mexico

Europe

イギリス	Igirisu	United Kingdom
イタリア	Itaria	Italy
オーストリア	Osutoria	Austria
オランダ	Oranda	Netherlands
ギリシャ	Girisha	Greece
スイス	Suisu	Switzerland
スウェーデン	Suwēden	Sweden
スペイン	Supein	Spain
デンマーク	Denmāku	Denmark
ドイツ	Doitsu	Germany
ノルウェー	Noruwē	Norway
フィンランド	Finrando	Finland
フランス	Furansu	France
ベルギー	Berugī	Belgium
ポーランド	Pōrando	Poland
ロシア	Roshia	Russia

Asia / Oceania

インド	Indo	India
インドネシア	Indoneshia	Indonesia
オーストラリア	Osutoraria	Australia
韓国 かんこく	Kankoku	Korea
サウジアラビア	Saujiarabia	Saudi Arabia
シンガポール	Shingapōru	Singapore
スリランカ	Suriranka	Sri Lanka
タイ	Tai	Thailand
台湾 たいわん	Taiwan	Taiwan
中国 ちゅうごく	Chūgoku	China

日本 にほん	Nihon	Japan
ニュージーランド	Nyūjīrando	New Zealand
ネパール	Nepāru	Nepal
バングラデシュ	Banguradeshu	Bangladesh
フィリピン	Firipin	Philippines
ベトナム	Betonamu	Vietnam
香港 ほんこん	Honkon	Hong Kong
マレーシア	Marēshia	Malaysia
ミャンマー	Myanmā	Myanmar
モンゴル	Mongoru	Mongolia

Africa / Middle East

アラブ首長国連邦 しゅちょうこくれんぽう Arabu shuchōkoku renpo		United Arab Emirates
アルジェリア	Arujeria	Algeria
イスラエル	Isuraeru	Israel
イラン	Iran	Iran
エジプト	Ejiputo	Egypt
トルコ	Toruko	Turkey
ナイジェリア	Naijeria	Nigeria
南アフリカ共和国 みなみ きょうわこく Minami Afurika kyōwakoku		Republic of South Africa

Jobs and Occupations
仕事と職業　しごと しょくぎょう　Shigoto to Shokugyō

会社員 かいしゃいん	kaishain	company employee
店員 てんいん	ten'in	clerk
エンジニア	enjinia	engineer
プログラマー	puroguramā	programmer
主婦 しゅふ	shufu	housewife
先生／教師 せんせい きょうし	sensei / kyōshi	teacher
医者 いしゃ	isha	doctor
公務員 こうむいん	kōmuin	public officials
研究者 けんきゅうしゃ	kenkyūsha	researcher
経営者 けいえいしゃ	keieisha	management
学生 がくせい	gakusei	student
高校生 こうこうせい	kōkōsei	high-school student
大学生 だいがくせい	daigakusei	college student
大学院生 だいがくいんせい	daigakuinsei	graduate student
留学生 りゅうがくせい	ryūgakusei	foreign students

School 学校 Gakkō

小学校	shōgakkō	elementary school
中学校	chūgakkō	junior high school
高校	kōkō	high schools
大学	daigaku	university
大学院	daigakuin	graduate school
1年生	ichi-nensei	first year
2年生	ni-nensei	second year
3年生	san-nensei	third year
4年生	yo-nensei	fourth year
教室	kyōshitsu	classroom
教科書	kyōkasho	textbook
宿題	shukudai	homework
テスト	tesuto	test, exam
レポート	repōto	report
学食	gakushoku	school cafeteria
経済学	keizaigaku	economics
政治学	seijigaku	political science
法学	hōgaku	law
社会学	shakaigaku	sociology
文学	bungaku	literature
工学	kōgaku	engineering
情報学	jōhōgaku	information science
化学	kagaku	chemistry
人類学	jinruigaku	anthropology
国際関係	kokusai-kankei	international relations
アジア研究	ajia-kenkyū	asian studies
ビジネス	bijinesu	business
コンピューターサイエンス konpyūtā-saiensu		computer science
ファッション	fasshon	fashion

Hobbies and Sports
趣味とスポーツ Shumi to Supōtsu

映画	eiga	movie
音楽	ongaku	music
読書	dokusho	reading books
旅行	ryokō	travel
写真	shashin	photo
買い物	kaimono	shopping
料理	ryōri	cooking
歌	uta	song
ゲーム	gēmu	game
まんが	manga	manga
アニメ	anime	animation
テレビ	terebi	tv
インターネット	intānetto	internet
サッカー	sakkā	soccer, football
野球	yakyū	baseball
バスケットボール	basukettobōru	basketball
テニス	tenisu	tennis
卓球	takkyū	table tennis
サーフィン	sāfin	surfing
スキー	sukī	skiing
スノーボード	sunōbōdo	snowboarding
ダンス	dansu	dance
ジョギング	jogingu	jogging
登山	tozan	climbing

Foods and Drinks
食べ物と飲み物 Tabemono to Nomimono

ご飯	gohan	rice
パン	pan	bread
魚	sakana	fish
肉	niku	meat
野菜	yasai	vegetables
すし	sushi	sushi
さしみ	sashimi	sashimi
焼き肉	yakiniku	roast
おにぎり	onigiri	rice ball
そば	soba	buckwheat noodles
うどん	udon	wheat noodles
牛丼	gyūdon	beef bowl
とんかつ	tonkatsu	pork cutlets
からあげ	kara'age	fried chicken
てんぷら	tenpura	tempura
ラーメン	rāmen	ramen
カレー	karē	curry
スパゲッティ	supagetthi	spaghetti
ピザ	piza	pizza
サンドイッチ	sandoicchi	sandwich
ハンバーガー	hanbāgā	hamburger
サラダ	sarada	salad
スープ	sūpu	soup
みそ汁	misoshiru	miso soup
砂糖	satō	sugar

塩	shio	salt
しょうゆ	shōyu	soy sauce
ソース	sōsu	source
日本料理／和食	Nihon-ryōri / washoku Japanese food	
中華料理	chūka-ryōri	Chinese food
デザート	dezāto	dessert
アイスクリーム	aisukurīmu	ice cream
ケーキ	kēki	cake
くだもの	kudamono	fruit
朝ご飯	asagohan	breakfast
昼ご飯	hirugohan	lunch
晩ご飯／夜ご飯	bangohan / yorugohan dinner	
（お）弁当	(o)bentō	lunch
水	mizu	water
（お）茶	(o)cha	tea
紅茶	kōcha	black tea
ウーロン茶	ūroncha	oolong tea
コーヒー	kōhī	coffee
ジュース	jūsu	juice
コーラ	kōra	cola
（お）酒	(o)sake	liquor
ビール	bīru	beer
ワイン	wain	wine

Shops and Facilities
店と施設　Mise to Shisetsu

レストラン	resutoran	restaurant
カフェ	kafe	cafe
コンビニ	konbini	convenience store
スーパー	sūpā	supermarket
薬局	yakkyoku	pharmacy
デパート	depāto	department store
電器屋	denkiya electric appliance store	
本屋	hon'ya	bookstore
銀行	ginkō	bank
郵便局	yūbinkyoku	post office
公園	kōen	park
神社	jinja	shrine
（お）寺	(o)tera	temple
ホテル	hoteru	hotel
旅館	ryokan	inn

映画館	eigakan	cinema
図書館	toshokan	library
病院	byōin	hospital
空港	kūkō	airport
学校	gakkō	school
自販機	jihanki	vending machine
お手洗い／トイレ	otearai / toire	restroom, toilet
入口	iriguchi	entrance
出口	deguchi	exit

Belongings　持ち物　Mochimono

ペン	pen	pen
ノート	nōto	notebook
電子辞書	denshijisho	electronic dictionary
パソコン	pasokon	personal computer
電話	denwa	phone
携帯（電話）	keitai(denwa)	mobile phone
電話番号	denwa-bangō	phone number
（メール）アドレス	(mēru)adoresu	(e-mail)address
カメラ	kamera	camera
傘	kasa	umbrella
さいふ	saifu	wallet

Clothing and Accessories
服とアクセサリー　Fuku to Akusesari

シャツ	shatsu	shirt
Tシャツ	tīshatsu	t-shirt
ジャケット	jaketto	jacket
コート	kōto	coat
ズボン／パンツ	zubon / pantsu	trousers, pants
スカート	sukāto	skirt
ジーンズ	jīnzu	jeans
くつ	kutsu	shoes
ぼうし	bōshi	hat
バッグ／かばん	baggu / kaban	bag
めがね	megane	glasses
時計	tokei	watch; clock

Body　体　Karada

頭	atama	head
髪	kami	head hair
顔	kao	face
目	me	eye
耳	mimi	ear

鼻 (はな)	hana	nose
口 (くち)	kuchi	mouth
歯 (は)	ha	tooth
首 (くび)	kubi	neck
肩 (かた)	kata	shoulder
腕 (うで)	ude	arm
手 (て)	te	hand
指 (ゆび)	yubi	finger
背中 (せなか)	senaka	back
腰 (こし)	koshi	lower back; waist
おなか	onaka	stomach
おしり	oshiri	hip
足 (あし)	ashi	leg; foot

Colors 色 (いろ) Iro

白(い) (しろ)	shiro(i)	white
黒(い) (くろ)	kuro(i)	black
赤(い) (あか)	aka(i)	red
青(い) (あお)	ao(i)	blue
黄色(い) (きいろ)	kiiro(i)	yellow
茶色(い) (ちゃいろ)	chairo(i)	brown
緑 (みどり)	midori	green
オレンジ	orenji	orange
ピンク	pinku	pink

Forms of Transportation 交通 (こうつう) Kōtsū

電車 (でんしゃ)	densha	electric train
地下鉄 (ちかてつ)	chikatetsu	subway
車 (くるま)	kuruma	car
バス	basu	bus
タクシー	takushī	taxi
新幹線 (しんかんせん)	shinkansen	bullet train
自転車 (じてんしゃ)	jitensha	bicycle
歩いて (ある)	aruite	on foot
バス停 (てい)	basutei	bus stop
駅 (えき)	eki	station
駐車場 (ちゅうしゃじょう)	chūshajō	parking lot
ガソリンスタンド	gasorinsutando	gas station
切符／チケット (きっぷ)	kippu / chiketto	ticket
飛行機 (ひこうき)	hikōki	airplane
船 (ふね)	fune	ship

Events イベント Ibento

(お)花見 (はな み)	(o)hanami	
		cherry-blossom viewing
花火 (はな び)	hanabi	fireworks
(お)祭り (まつ)	(o)matsuri	a festival
(お)正月 (しょうがつ)	(o)shōgatsu	New Year's
クリスマス	kurisumasu	christmas
コンサート	konsāto	concert
パーティー	pātī	party
カラオケ	karaoke	karaoke
飲み放題 (の ほうだい)	nomihōdai	all you can drink
食べ放題 (た ほうだい)	tabehōdai	all you can eat

Weather and Nature 天気と自然 (てんき しぜん) Tenki to Shizen

春 (はる)	haru	spring
夏 (なつ)	natsu	summer
秋 (あき)	aki	fall
冬 (ふゆ)	fuyu	winter
晴れ (は)	hare	sunny
くもり	kumori	cloudy
雨 (あめ)	ame	rain
風 (かぜ)	kaze	wind
雪 (ゆき)	yuki	snow
雷 (かみなり)	kaminari	thunder
台風 (たいふう)	taifū	typhoon
地震 (じ しん)	jishin	earthquake
山 (やま)	yama	mountain
川 (かわ)	kawa	river
海 (うみ)	umi	sea
温泉 (おんせん)	onsen	hot springs

Directions and Positions 方向と位置 (ほうこう い ち) Hōkō to Ichi

東 (ひがし)	higashi	east
西 (にし)	nishi	west
北 (きた)	kita	north
南 (みなみ)	minami	south
上 (うえ)	ue	higher; up; on; above
下 (した)	shita	lower; down; under; below
中 (なか)	naka	in; inside
外 (そと)	soto	out; outside

近く	chikaku	nearby
となり	tonari	next (to one)
前	mae	front; forward
後ろ	ushiro	back; behind
右	migi	right
左	hidari	left

Common Verbs
よく使う動詞　Yoku tsukau dōshi

あげます／あげる(II)　agemasu / ageru	give
会います／会う(I)　aimasu / au	meet
開けます／開ける(II)　akemasu / akeru	open
洗います／洗う(I)　araimasu / arau	wash
あります／ある(I)　arimasu / aru	be (thing)
遊びます／遊ぶ(I)　asobimasu / asobu (I)	play
勉強します／勉強する(III)　benkyō shimaru / benkyō suru	study; learn
電話します／電話する(III)　denwa shimasu / denwa suru	call, telephone
始まります／始まる(I)　hajimarimasu / hajimaru	start
話します／話す(I)　hanashimasu / hanasu	talk; speak
払います／払う(I)　haraimasu / harau	pay
働きます／働く(I)　hatarakimasu / hataraku	work
言います／言う(I)　iimasu / iu	say
行きます／行く(I)　ikimasu / iku	go
います／いる(II)　imasu / iru	be (person, animal)
いります／いる(I)　irimasu / iru	need
急ぎます／急ぐ(I)　isogimasu / isogu	hurry; rush
準備します／準備する(III)　junbi shimasu / junbi suru	prepare
帰ります／帰る(I)　kaerimasu / kaeru	return
買います／買う(I)　kaimasu / kau	buy
書きます／書く(I)　kakimasu / kaku	write
考えます／考える(II)　kangaemasu / kangaeru	think
借ります／借りる(II)　karimasu / kariru	rent
貸します／貸す(I)　kashimasu / kasu	lend

結婚します／結婚する(III)　kekkon shimasu / kekkon suru	marry
消します／消す(I)　keshimasu / kesu	turn off
聞きます／聞く(I)　kikimasu / kiku	listen; hear; ask
着ます／着る(II)　kimasu / kiru	wear
来ます／来る(III)　kimasu / kuru	come
答えます／答える(II)　kotaemasu / kotaeru	answer
待ちます／待つ(I)　machimasu / matsu	wait
メールします／メールする(III)　mēru shimasu / mēru suru	send e-mail
見ます／見る(II)　mimasu / miru	see; look; watch
見せます／見せる(II)　misemasu / miseru	show
もらいます／もらう(I)　moraimasu / morau	receive; get
持っていきます／持っていく　motte'ikimasu / motte'iku	take, carry
持ってきます／持ってくる(III)　mottekimasu / mottekuru	bring (things)
なります／なる(I)　narimasu / naru	become
寝ます／寝る(II)　nemasu / neru	go to bed; sleep
飲みます／飲む(I)　nomimasu / nomu	drink
乗ります／乗る(I)　norimasu / noru	ride; get on
覚えます／覚える(II)　oboemasu / oboeru	remember; keep in mind
起きます／起きる(II)　okimasu / okiru	get up
送ります／送る(I)　okurimasu / okuru	send
思います／思う(I)　omoimasu / omou	think; guess
降ります／降りる(II)　orimasu / oriru	get off; go down
教えます／教える(II)　oshiemasu / oshieru	teach
終わります／終わる(I)　owarimasu / owaru	finish
連絡します／連絡する(III)　renraku shimasu / renraku suru	contact
練習します／練習する(III)　renshū shimasu / renshū suru	practice
留学します／留学する(III)　ryūgaku shimasu / ryūgaku suru	study abroad
します／する(III)　shimasu / suru	do

Japanese	Romaji	English
閉めます／閉める（Ⅱ） shimemasu / shimeru		close
質問します／質問する（Ⅲ） shitsumon shimasu / shitsumon suru		ask, question
知っています／知っている（Ⅱ）* shitte'imasu / shitte'iru		know
そうじします／そうじする（Ⅲ） sōji shimasu / sōji suru		clean
卒業します／卒業する（Ⅲ） sotsugyō shimasu / sotsugyō suru		graduate
住んでいます／住んでいる（Ⅱ）* sunde'imasu / sunde'iru		live
座ります／座る（Ⅰ） suwarimasu / suwaru		sit
食べます／食べる（Ⅱ） tabemasu / taberu		eat
立ちます／立つ（Ⅰ） tachimasu / tatsu		stand
手伝います／手伝う（Ⅰ） tetsudaimasu / tetsudau		help
泊まります／泊まる（Ⅰ） tomarimasu / tomaru		stay
取ります／取る（Ⅰ）　torimasu / toru		take
撮ります／撮る（Ⅰ）　torimasu / toru		take (photos)
使います／使う（Ⅰ） tsukaimasu / tsukau		use
作ります／作る（Ⅰ） tsukurimasu / tsukuru		make
つけます／つける（Ⅱ） tsukemasu / tsukeru		put; turn on
歌います／歌う（Ⅰ） utaimasu / utau		sing
わかります／わかる（Ⅰ） wakarimasu / wakaru		understand; know
忘れます／忘れる（Ⅱ） wasuremasu / wasureru		forget
休みます／休む（Ⅰ） yasumimasu / yasumu		take a rest; be absent
呼びます／呼ぶ（Ⅰ） yobimasu / yobu		call
読みます／読む（Ⅰ） yomimasu / yomu		read
予約します／予約する（Ⅲ） yoyaku shimasu / yoyaku suru		reserve

*"shitte'imasu" and "sunde'imasu" are special forms, so remember to take note of their respective meanings when you use them in conversation.

Common Adjectives
よく使う形容詞　Yoku tsukau keiyōshi

大きい	ōkii	big; large
小さい	chiisai	small
いい	ii	good
悪い	warui	bad
新しい	atarashii	new
古い	furui	old
高い	takai	high, tall; expensive (price)
低い	hikui	low
安い	yasui	cheap
早い	hayai	early
速い	hayai	fast
遅い	osoi	slow
長い	nagai	long
短い	mijikai	short
簡単（な）	kantan (na)	easy
難しい	muzukashii	difficult
遠い	tōi	far, distant
近い	chikai	close, near
上手（な）	jōzu (na)	good
下手（な）	heta (na)	poor
暑い	atsui	hot (weather)
寒い	samui	cold (weather)
熱い	atsui	hot (object)
冷たい	tsumetai	cold (object)
すずしい	suzushii	cool
あたたかい	atatakai	warm
きれい（な）	kirei (na)	pretty; clean
きたない	kitanai	dirty
うるさい	urusai	noisy
しずか（な）	shizuka (na)	quiet
忙しい	isogashii	busy
ひま（な）	hima (na)	free time
おもしろい	omoshiroi	funny; interesting
つまらない	tsumaranai	boring
おいしい	oishii	delicious
楽しい	tanoshii	fun
すごい	sugoi	amazing, incredible
かっこいい	kakkoii	cool
かわいい	kawaii	cute
ねむい	nemui	sleepy
こわい	kowai	scary
わかい	wakai	young
ほしい	hoshii	want

好き（な）	suki(na)	like	だれ	dare	who
大好き（な）	daisuki(na)	love	いつ	itsu	when
元気（な）	genki(na)	healthy；happy	どうして／なんで	dōshite / nande	why
親切（な）	shinsetsu(na)	helpful；kind	どんな	donna	what
大変（な）	taihen(na)	very	どう	dō	what
便利（な）	benri(na)	convenient	どのぐらい	donogurai	how long
すてき（な）	suteki(na)	nice；wonderful	どうやって	dōyatte	how
有名（な）	yūmei(na)	famous	いくら	ikura	how much
大切（な）	taisetsu(na)	important	いくつ	ikutsu	how many
変（な）	hen(na)	strange	何人	nan-nin	how many people

Interrogatives　疑問詞　Gimonshi

			何年生	nan-nensei	what year in school
何	nani / nan	what	何歳	nan-sai	how old
どこ	doko	where	何階	nan-kai	what floor
			何色	nani-iro	what color

Counter suffix　助数詞　Josūshi

	～個 (for small things)	～枚 (for paper, clothing, etc.)	～本 (for pen, bottle, etc.)	～回 (for number of times)
1	いっこ ikko	いちまい ichi-nichi	いっぽん ippon	いっかい ikkai
2	にこ ni-ko	にまい ni-mai	にほん ni-hon	にかい ni-kai
3	さんこ san-ko	さんまい san-mai	さんぼん san-bon	さんかい san-kai
4	よんこ yon-ko	よんまい yon-mai	よんほん yon-hon	よんかい yon-kai
：				
？ 何	なんこ nan-ko	なんまい nan-mai	なんぼん nan-bon	なんかい nan-kai

Calendar　カレンダー　Karendā

Months　～月

？ 何月　nan-gatsu

1　January いちがつ ichi-gatsu	2　Februaly にがつ ni-gatsu	3　March さんがつ san-gatsu	4　April しがつ shi-gatsu	5　May ごがつ go-gatsu	6　June ろくがつ roku-gatsu
7　July しちがつ shichi-gatsu	8　August はちがつ hachi-gatsu	9　September くがつ ku-gatsu	10　October じゅうがつ jū-gatsu	11　November じゅういちがつ jūichi-gatsu	12　December じゅうにがつ jūni-gatsu

Dates　～日／日

？ 何日　nan-nichi

1 ついたち tuitachi	2 ふつか futsuka	3 みっか mikka	4 よっか yokka	5 いつか itsuka	6 むいか muika	7 なのか nanoka
8 ようか yōka	9 ここのか kokonoka	10 とおか tōka	11 じゅういちにち jūichi-nichi	12 じゅうににち jūni-nichi	13 じゅうさんにち jūsan-nichi	14 じゅうよっか jūyokka
15 じゅうごにち jūgo-nichi	16 じゅうろくにち jūroku-nichi	17 じゅうしちにち jūshichi-nichi	18 じゅうはちにち jūhachi-nichi	19 じゅうくにち jūku-nichi	20 はつか hatsuka	21 にじゅういちにち nijūichi-nichi
22 にじゅうににち nijūni-nichi	23 にじゅうさんにち nijūsan-nichi	24 にじゅうよっか nijūyokka	25 にじゅうごにち nijūgo-nichi	26 にじゅうろくにち nijūroku-nichi	27 にじゅうしちにち nijūshichi-nichi	28 にじゅうはちにち nijūhachi-nichi
29 にじゅうくにち nijūku-nichi	30 さんじゅうにち sanjū-nichi	31 さんじゅういちにち sanjūichi-nichi				

Days　～曜日

？ 何曜日　nan-yōbi

Sunday にちようび 日曜日 nichi-yōbi	Monday げつようび 月曜日 getsu-yōbi	Tuesday かようび 火曜日 ka-yōbi	Wednesday すいようび 水曜日 sui-yōbi	Thursday もくようび 木曜日 moku-yōbi	Friday きんようび 金曜日 kin-yōbi	Saturday どようび 土曜日 do-yōbi

Time course

	Before last	Last	This	Next	After next	Every
Day	おととい 一昨日 ototoi	きのう 昨日 kinō	きょう 今日 kyō	あした 明日 ashita	あさって 明後日 asatte	まいにち 毎日 mainichi
Week	せんせんしゅう 先々週 sensenshū	せんしゅう 先週 senshū	こんしゅう 今週 konshū	らいしゅう 来週 raishū	さらいしゅう 再来週 saraishū	まいしゅう 毎週 maishū
Month	せんせんげつ 先々月 sensengetsu	せんげつ 先月 sengetsu	こんげつ 今月 kongetsu	らいげつ 来月 raigetsu	さらいげつ 再来月 saraigetsu	まいつき 毎月 maitsuki
Year	おととし 一昨年 ototoshi	きょねん 去年 kyonen	ことし 今年 kotoshi	らいねん 来年 rainen	さらいねん 再来年 sarainen	まいとし 毎年 maitoshi

Time and Duration
時間と期間　Jikan to Kikan

Time

	Time 〜時	Minutes 〜分
1	いちじ　ichi-ji	いっぷん　ippun
2	にじ　ni-ji	にふん　ni-fun
3	さんじ　san-ji	さんぷん　san-pun
4	よじ　yo-ji	よんぷん　yon-pun
5	ごじ　go-ji	ごふん　go-fun
6	ろくじ　roku-ji	ろっぷん　roppun
7	しちじ　shichi-ji	ななふん　nana-fun
8	はちじ　hachi-ji	はっぷん　happun
9	くじ　ku-ji	きゅうふん　kyū-fun
10	じゅうじ　jū-ji	じゅっぷん　juppun
11	じゅういちじ　jūichi-ji	じゅういっぷん　jūippun
12	じゅうにじ　jūni-ji	じゅうにふん　jūni-fun
? 何	なんじ　nan-ji	なんぷん　nan-pun

Ex. 11:00 a.m.　午前 11 時　　　　　　gozen jūichi-ji
　　3:30 p.m.　午後 3 時 30 分／3 時半　gogo san-ji sanjuppun / san-ji-han

Duration

	Hour 〜時間	Day 〜日(間)	Week 〜週間	Month 〜か月(間)	Year 〜年(間)
1	いちじかん ichi-jikan	いちにち ichi-nichi	いっしゅうかん isshūkan	いっかげつ(かん) ikkagetsu(kan)	いちねん(かん) ichi-nen(kan)
2	にじかん ni-jikan	ふつか(かん) futsuka(kan)	にしゅうかん ni-shūkan	にかげつ(かん) ni-kagetsu(kan)	にねん(かん) ni-nen(kan)
3	さんじかん san-jikan	みっか(かん) mikka(kan)	さんしゅうかん san-shūkan	さんかげつ(かん) san-kagetsu(kan)	さんねん(かん) san-nen(kan)
4	よじかん yo-jikan	よっか(かん) yokka(kan)	よんしゅうかん yon-shūkan	よんかげつ(かん) yon-kagetsu(kan)	よねん(かん) yo-nen(kan)
:					
? 何	なんじかん nan-jikan	なんにち(かん) nan-nichi(kan)	なんしゅうかん nan-shūkan	なんかげつ(かん) nan-kagetsu(kan)	なんねん(かん) nan-nen(kan)

The Districts of Japan
日本の地域　Nihon no Chiiki

1	北海道	Hokkaido

2	青森県	Aomori-ken
3	岩手県	Iwate-ken
4	秋田県	Akita-ken
5	宮城県	Miyagi-ken
6	山形県	Yamagata-ken
7	福島県	Fukushima-ken

東北地方
Tōhoku-chihō

15	新潟県	Nīgata-ken
16	富山県	Toyama-ken
17	石川県	Ishikawa-ken
18	福井県	Fukui-ken
19	長野県	Nagano-ken
20	岐阜県	Gifu-ken
21	山梨県	Yamanashi-ken
22	静岡県	Shizuoka-ken
23	愛知県	Aichi-ken

中部地方
Chūbu-chihō

31	鳥取県	Tottori-ken
32	島根県	Shimane-ken
33	岡山県	Okayama-ken
34	広島県	Hiroshima-ken
35	山口県	Yamaguchi-ken

中国地方
Chūgoku-chihō

36	徳島県	Tokushima-ken
37	香川県	Kagawa-ken
38	高知県	Kōchi-ken
39	愛媛県	Ehime-ken

四国地方
Shikoku-chihō

40	福岡県	Fukuoka-ken
41	佐賀県	Saga-ken
42	長崎県	Nagasaki-ken
43	大分県	Ōita-ken
44	熊本県	Kumamoto-ken
45	宮崎県	Miyazaki-ken
46	鹿児島県	Kagoshima-ken

九州地方
Kyūshū-chihō

47	沖縄県	Okinawa-ken

8	茨城県	Ibaraki-ken
9	栃木県	Tochigi-ken
10	群馬県	Gunma-ken
11	埼玉県	Saitama-ken
12	千葉県	Chiba-ken
13	東京都	Tōkyō-to
14	神奈川県	Kanagawa-ken

関東地方
Kantō-chihō

24	三重県	Mie-ken
25	滋賀県	Shiga-ken
26	京都府	Kyōto-fu
27	兵庫県	Hyōgo-ken
28	奈良県	Nara-ken
29	和歌山県	Wakayama-ken
30	大阪府	Ōsaka-fu

近畿地方
Kinki-chihō

日光 Nikkō

富士山 Fuji-san

原爆ドーム Genbaku Dōmu

16

Verb Conjugation List

Group Ⅰ

Masu-form	Dictionary form	Te-form	Ta-form	Nai-form	Meaning
あいます aimasu	あう au	あって atte	あった atta	あわない awanai	meet
あります arimasu	ある aru	あって atte	あった atta	ない* nai	be（thing）
ちがいます chigaimasu	ちがう chigau	ちがって chigatte	ちがった chigatta	ちがわない chigawanai	be different
はなします hanashimasu	はなす hanasu	はなして hanashite	はなした hanashita	はなさない hanasanai	talk；speak
はたらきます hatarakimasu	はたらく hataraku	はたらいて hataraite	はたらいた hataraita	はたらかない hatarakanai	work
いきます ikimasu	いく iku	いって itte	いった itta	いかない ikanai	go
いいます iimasu	いう iu	いって itte	いった itta	いわない iwanai	say
かえります kaerimasu	かえる kaeru	かえって kaette	かえった kaetta	かえらない kaeranai	return
かいます kaimasu	かう kau	かって katte	かった katta	かわない kawanai	buy
かかります kakarimasu	かかる kakaru	かかって kakatte	かかった kakatta	かからない kakaranai	take（time）
かきます kakimasu	かく kaku	かいて kaite	かいた kaita	かかない kakanai	write
けします keshimasu	けす kesu	けして keshite	けした keshita	けさない kesanai	turn off
ききます kikimasu	きく kiku	きいて kiite	きいた kiita	きかない kikanai	listen；hear；ask
まちます machimasu	まつ matsu	まって matte	まった matta	またない matanai	wait
まがります magarimasu	まがる magaru	まがって magatte	まがった magatta	まがらない magaranai	turn
もらいます moraimasu	もらう morau	もらって moratte	もらった moratta	もらわない morawanai	receive；get
のみます nomimasu	のむ nomu	のんで nonde	のんだ nonda	のまない nomanai	drink
のります norimasu	のる norimasu	のって notte	のった notta	のらない noranai	ride；get on
おくります okurimasu	おくる okuru	おくって okutte	おくった okutta	おくらない okuranai	send
おもいます omoimasu	おもう omou	おもって omotte	おもった omotta	おもわない omowanai	think
すわります suwarimasu	すわる suwaru	すわって suwatte	すわった suwatta	すわらない suwaranai	sit
てつだいます tetsudaimasu	てつだう tetsudau	てつだって tetsudatte	てつだった tetsudatta	てつだわない tetsudawanai	help

＊The nai-form of "*arimasu*" is "*nai*".

とまります tomarimasu	とまる tomaru	とまって tomatte	とまった tomatta	とまらない tomaranai	stay; stop
とります torimasu	とる toru	とって totte	とった totta	とらない toranai	take (things, photos)
つかいます tsukaimasu	つかう tsukau	つかって tsukatte	つかった tsukatta	つかわない tsukawanai	use
つくります tsukurimasu	つくる tsukuru	つくって tsukutte	つくった tsukutta	つくらない tsukuranai	make
わかります wakarimasu	わかる wakaru	わかって wakatte	わかった wakatta	わからない wakaranai	understand; know
やすみます yasumimasu	やすむ yasumu	やすんで yasunde	やすんだ yasunda	やすまない yasumanai	take a rest; be absent
よみます yomimasu	よむ yomu	よんで yonde	よんだ yonda	よまない yomanai	read

Group Ⅱ

Masu-form	Dictionary form	Te-form	Ta-form	Nai-form	Meaning
あげます agemasu	あげる ageru	あげて agete	あげた ageta	あげない agenai	give
います imasu	いる iru	いて ite	いた ita	いない inai	be (person, animal)
いれます iremasu	いれる ireru	いれて irete	いれた ireta	いれない irenai	enter; put in
きます kimasu	きる kiru	きて kite	きた kita	きない kinai	put on (clothing)
みます mimasu	みる miru	みて mite	みた mita	みない minai	see; look; watch
みせます misemasu	みせる miseru	みせて misete	みせた miseta	みせない misenai	show
ねます nemasu	ねる neru	ねて nete	ねた neta	ねない nenai	go to bed; sleep
おぼえます oboemasu	おぼえる oboeru	おぼえて oboete	おぼえた oboeta	おぼえない oboenai	remember; keep in mind
おきます okimasu	おきる okiru	おきて okite	おきた okita	おきない okinai	get up
おります orimasu	おりる oriru	おりて orite	おりた orita	おりない orinai	get off; go down
おしえます oshiemasu	おしえる oshieru	おしえて oshiete	おしえた oshieta	おしえない oshienai	teach
たべます tabemasu	たべる taberu	たべて tabete	たべた tabeta	たべない tabenai	eat
つけます tsukemasu	つける tsukeru	つけて tsukete	つけた tsuketa	つけない tsukenai	turn on
わすれます wasuremasu	わすれる wasureru	わすれて wasurete	わすれた wasureta	わすれない wasurenai	forget

Group Ⅲ

Masu-form	Dictionary form	Te-form	Ta-form	Nai-form	Meaning
べんきょうします benkyō shimasu	べんきょうする benkyō suru	べんきょうして benkyō shite	べんきょうした benkyō shita	べんきょうしない benkyō shinai	study; learn
でんわします denwa shimasu	でんわする denwa suru	でんわして denwa shite	でんわした denwa shita	でんわしない denwa shinai	call, telephone
きます kimasu	くる kuru	きて kite	きた kita	こない konai	come
メールします mēru shimasu	メールする mēru suru	メールして mēru shite	メールした mēru shita	メールしない mēru shinai	send e-mail
もってきます mottekimasu	もってくる mottekuru	もってきて mottekite	もってきた mottekita	もってこない mottekonai	bring (things)
れんらくします renraku shimasu	れんらくする renraku suru	れんらくして renraku shite	れんらくした renraku shita	れんらくしない renraku shinai	contact
れんしゅうします renshū shimasu	れんしゅうする renshū suru	れんしゅうして renshū shite	れんしゅうした renshū shita	れんしゅうしない renshū shinai	practice
します shimasu	する suru	して shite	した shita	しない shinai	do
よやくします yoyaku shimasu	よやくする yoyaku suru	よやくして yoyaku shite	よやくした yoyaku shita	よやくしない yoyaku shinai	reserve